a SAVOR THE SOUTH *cookbook*

Shrimp

SAVOR THE SOUTH *cookbooks*

Rice, by Michael W. Twitty (2021)

Pie, by Sara Foster (2018)

Ham, by Damon Lee Fowler (2017)

Corn, by Tema Flanagan (2017)

Fruit, by Nancie McDermott (2017)

Chicken, by Cynthia Graubart (2016)

Bacon, by Fred Thompson (2016)

Greens, by Thomas Head (2016)

Barbecue, by John Shelton Reed (2016)

Crabs and Oysters, by Bill Smith (2015)

Sunday Dinner, by Bridgette A. Lacy (2015)

Beans and Field Peas, by Sandra A. Gutierrez (2015)

Gumbo, by Dale Curry (2015)

Shrimp, by Jay Pierce (2015)

Catfish, by Paul and Angela Knipple (2015)

Sweet Potatoes, by April McGreger (2014)

Southern Holidays, by Debbie Moose (2014)

Okra, by Virginia Willis (2014)

Pickles and Preserves, by Andrea Weigl (2014)

Bourbon, by Kathleen Purvis (2013)

Biscuits, by Belinda Ellis (2013)

Tomatoes, by Miriam Rubin (2013)

Peaches, by Kelly Alexander (2013)

Pecans, by Kathleen Purvis (2012)

Buttermilk, by Debbie Moose (2012)

a SAVOR THE SOUTH *cookbook*

Shrimp

JAY PIERCE

The University of North Carolina Press CHAPEL HILL

The paper in this book meets the guidelines for permanence and durability of
the Committee on Production Guidelines for Book Longevity of the Council on
Library Resources.

Cover illustration: depositphotos.com/© koosen

Library of Congress Cataloging-in-Publication Data
Pierce, Jay (Chef)
Shrimp / by Jay Pierce.
pages cm.—(Savor the South cookbooks)
Includes index.
ISBN 978-1-4696-2114-2 (cloth : alk. paper)
ISBN 978-1-4696-7760-6 (pbk. : alk. paper)
ISBN 978-1-4696-2115-9 (ebook)
1. Cooking (Shrimp) 2. Cooking, American—Southern style. I. Title.
TX754.S58P54 2015   641.6′95—dc23
2014023109

New Orleans–Style Barbecue Shrimp in South Carolina; Tom Yum Goong, a
Thai Shrimp Soup; and Buttered Brown Rice with Shrimp, Duck Cracklings,
and Roasted Mushrooms are based on recipes in Joe and Heidi Trull, *Grits and
Groceries: Real Food Done Real Good* (Belton, S.C., 2007); Nancie McDermott,
Real Thai: The Best of Thailand's Regional Cooking (San Francisco: Chronicle
Books, 1992); and Gabrielle Hamilton, *Prune* (New York: Random House, forth-
coming), respectively.

Contents

INTRODUCTION Shrimp Matters 1

Small Plates 15
Bacon-Wrapped Shrimp Brochettes with Rhubarbecue Sauce 16
Salt-and-Pepper Shrimp 18
Shrimp and Leek Quiche 20
Bertie County Company Shrimp and Crackers 22
Shrimp with Cocktail Sauce 24
Saucy Cocktail with Shrimp 26
Shrimp Ceviche 28
Shrimp Aspic 30
Shrimp Omelet 32
Prized Pickled Shrimp 33
Coconut Fried Shrimp with Mango-Teriyaki Sauce 34
New Orleans–Style Barbecue Shrimp in South Carolina 36

Salads 39
Grilled Shrimp Caesar Salad 40
Popcorn Shrimp Rémoulade Salad 42
Shrimp and Peach Salad 44
Roasted Shrimp Salad 45

Soups 47
Seafood Gumbo 48
Cream of Fennel Soup with Shrimp 50
Mirliton and Shrimp Soup 52

Tom Yum Goong, a Thai Shrimp Soup 54

Rosemary Shrimp and White Bean Soup 56

Brandied Shrimp Bisque 58

Sweet Potato Soup with Ginger Shrimp 60

With Your Hands 63

Classic Fried Shrimp Po'boys 64

Fire-Roasted Shrimp Tacos 66

Gulf Shrimp Rolls 68

Shrimp Burgers with Boiler Room Tartar Sauce,
Tomatoes, and Arugula 70

With Noodles 73

Garlicky Shrimp with Angel Hair Pasta 74

Calabash Cajun Carbonara 76

Shrimp Linguine 78

With Rice 81

Jambalaya 82

Shrimp Country Captain 84

Creamed Rice with Spicy Sausage and Shrimp 86

Buttered Brown Rice with Shrimp, Duck Cracklings,
and Roasted Mushrooms 88

Lemony Shrimp Risotto 90

Shrimp and Okra 92

Esma's Shrimp Stew 94

Shrimp Étouffée 96

Composed Dishes 99

Shrimp and Spinach Enchiladas 100

Cajun Shrimp Boil 102

Grilled Steaks with Shrimp Butter 104

Shrimp-Stuffed Pork Chops 106

Southwestern Shrimp Stew 108

Shrimp and Grits 109

Acknowledgments 112   *Index 113*

a SAVOR THE SOUTH *cookbook*

Shrimp

Introduction

SHRIMP MATTERS

njoyed equally at the finest white-tablecloth celebrations and when eaten with bare hands in sundrenched locales, shrimp have an unending versatility that may very well make them the perfect food. The most consumed seafood in America, shrimp can be found on menus coast to coast, but southerners enjoy a special relationship with shrimp dishes. Whether due to our proximity to shrimp-abundant waters or the tremendous influence of our French, Spanish, and African forebears on our foodways, a truly southern menu isn't complete without a beloved shrimp dish.

From seersucker suits to chess pies, from whole hog cookery to SEC football, the South is in style. A paramount southern delicacy, shrimp are eaten with gusto in coastal communities and at potlucks and other gatherings to celebrate family reunions, engagements, weddings, christenings, and wakes. Shrimp cookery is easy to learn, and shrimp can be seasoned to suit a wide range of tastes. A lean protein that's mildly sweet, these tasty crustaceans can be incorporated into almost any dish, from enchiladas to spaghetti, po'boys to ceviche, Thai curry to bloody marys. And how can you beat entertaining a crowd with a pure and simple shrimp boil? While these crustaceans are still ubiquitous throughout the country in the uninspired shrimp cocktails of generic hotel restaurants or the fried shrimp baskets of fast-food outlets, southern chefs and home cooks alike have embraced the myriad ways that shrimp can be brought to the table. The past decade has seen numerous interesting incarnations of shrimp and grits, showcasing that southern triumvirate of pork, seafood, and grits and paying tribute to the local crustaceans in a way that elevates shrimp above all other seafood. Whereas crawfish can be an acquired taste beyond South Louisiana and crabs require a lot of work to yield those succulent hunks of meat, shrimp are approachable, easy to manipulate, and just plain delectable. And shrimp are downright irreplaceable in the South. Seafood gumbo wouldn't be a quintessential southern dish if it didn't include shrimp—crab stock provides the backbone, but shrimp provide the sex appeal that beckons you hither.

Is there a more delightful taste surprise than the one you get when sitting at a newspaper-covered picnic table in someone's backyard with the sun shining through your heavily tinted sunglasses; the air thick with humidity; a sweating, icy-cold beer in your hand; and the tender flesh of a shrimp giving way with a pop between your teeth? Your anticipation transports you to a timeless place where you commune with your ancestors, who also participated in this ritual for years untold. The wafting aromas of cayenne pepper, garlic, and brine make your heart race. Between the spicy andouille sausage, the Silver Queen corn, and the mounds of colorful crustaceans, your senses are overwhelmed. Your fingers and lips burn from the heat and the spice, and the only thing that limits your intake is how fast you can peel.

But What Do I Know?

Growing up on the Louisiana Gulf Coast, I had many occasions to catch, sort, buy, dehead, peel, freeze, thaw, devein, and cook shrimp, from brown shrimp in May to white shrimp in August. Every family that I knew growing up had enough bags of shrimp in the freezer to last until the next shrimp season. Prior to the invention of resealable freezer bags, repurposed margarine containers were employed, which had in turn replaced half-gallon wax milk cartons; folks would peel apart the back of the spout to form a square opening at the top of the carton. Every family knew more than a community-cookbookful of ways to prepare its Gulf shrimp—way more than just fried shrimp and shrimp cocktail.

When I was a kid, sometimes my dad would take me trawling for shrimp. I remember having to get up so early that it still felt like it was the night before. The goal was to pack everything before we went to sleep, wake up, make sandwiches (ham and American cheese with Blue Plate mayonnaise), drive down to

Myrtle Grove (about thirty minutes away), and be in the boat and on the water before the sun came up. When picturing shrimpers at work, most folks think of commercial fishing vessels with their huge butterfly nets on outriggers hoisted into the sky, but recreational trawlers that work inland waterways are a bit different. We would set out in a twenty-foot boat with a sixteen-foot-long funnel-shaped net, wide at the stern of the boat and tapering to a narrow opening that was tied closed. The mouth of the net was attached to empty milk jugs or floats at the top and weighted at the bottom with a chain. The net was held open as the boat moved slowly through the water by the hydrodynamic force on the metal-reinforced oak boards that flanked the opening. Everything in the boat's path that couldn't swim fast enough to get out of the way was consumed by the maw of this net. Another float was affixed to the trailing end of the net (referred to as the "ball" when full). I didn't know it then, but this type of net is known as an otter trawl, and its adoption by shrimpers in the early twentieth century had a profound impact on the commercial shrimping industry in the South.

In the boat, my dad would attempt to aim the boat where the shrimp might be, cutting the wheel back and forth so we would proceed in a serpentine pattern. We would always hope to find a "jubilee," which is when the shrimp are at the surface of the water, feeding and splashing and just asking to be caught. From the dock, we would motor down Wilkinson Canal to get to Little Lake or Lake Salvador or whichever body of water we wanted to try that Saturday morning. My dad would make a pass for about an hour or so and then pull in the "lazy line" to bring the ball closer to the boat to see if we were catching anything. If the ball had more shrimp than mud, he'd kill the engine and we'd pull in the lines to collect the net. On a good day when the net was full, this would be a chore. After the whole net was pulled into the boat, the ball was placed in the picking box and opened. All manner of creatures would spill out into that plywood trough arranged across the gunwales. Next would come my primary responsibility: sorting through the catch, throwing overboard the small fish, sticks, mud clods, jellyfish, and other undesirable bycatch. We would usually score some flounder or other bottom-dwelling fish, and we would always get crabs, which would go into a separate hamper. Once the catch was reduced to just shrimp, we would place them in ice chests. Meanwhile, my dad would be dragging the net again as I was picking, and if we were in the right place at the right time, it would be time to haul in the net by the time I was done in the picking box. This would go on for a few hours until we would stop to eat our sandwiches, then we would take the boat into dock and drive home with our catch. We would get home around noon, smelly and tired, but our work for the day wasn't done yet. We still had to sort the shrimp, pop the heads off, and freeze them. We would sell some to neighbors and have some for dinner that night. Our freezer would be packed with enough shrimp to eat weekly for the next six months or so.

Familiarity Breeds Contempt

Having a freezer full of a particular food can spawn bouts of creativity that would rival the oft-parodied scene from the film *Forrest Gump*, in which a character monotonously drones on about all of the dishes one can create with shrimp. Eating shrimp at our house most often meant pulling a container or bag from the freezer to thaw for most of the day. Peeling off the shells and rinsing the glistening tails always fell to the person cooking dinner (no prep crew here). Next, the cook would have to decide whether the shrimp would star in a garlicky, buttery pasta or be added to jambalaya or spaghetti, deep-fried for sandwiches, baked in the oven as "New Orleans barbecue," or boiled. On the days we caught shrimp, boiling often won out because boiling is best done with fresh, unfrozen, head-on, shell-on shrimp. The person eating, rather than the cook, cleans the shrimp.

When we didn't have a boat to go trawling, we had two options for filling our freezer with shrimp. My dad could go shrimping on a bigger boat and split the catch with the other guys on board, but this was the same amount of work as trawling for shrimp ourselves, or more, with less of a payoff. Or we could always find someone, often one of our neighbors, who was selling shrimp, perhaps out of a pickup truck under a highway overpass (just like the watermelon man in his season), or in the "shrimp lot" in Westwego. This was an empty lot where shrimpers would park their trucks and sell the day's catch out of huge ice chests, using scales and colorful signs advertising their prices. This was my first encounter with the local food movement—before it was a movement, it was a way of life. If you wanted shrimp, you caught them or bought them from someone who caught them. The same went for fish or crabs or crawfish. And talk about fresh. Sometimes the legs were still kicking when you scooped them out of the shrimpers' ice chests.

What Is a Shrimp?

Shrimp are decapod (Greek for ten-footed) crustaceans that are spawned in open salt water and ride the tide into estuaries and marshes, where they overcome the awkward teenage stage. Then they swim out into bays and oceans to frolic and mate and begin the lifecycle over again. Since this is a yearly cycle, shrimp fisheries are considered sustainable because they're self-renewing. Humans must manage shrimp habitats to ensure next year's crop. This includes closing fisheries to harvesting at certain times of the year and monitoring agricultural runoff and environmental conditions.

The edible part of the shrimp, as with other crustaceans, is its meaty, very lean tail section. Because the majority of the animal's flavorful fat is in the head segment, shrimp retain more of their shrimpness when cooked intact in the shell. Not only is the tender flesh protected from the cooking medium, whether it be flame or simmering liquid, but the body fat in the head helps keep the tail meat moist. (Remember to save those shells in your freezer for when you want to make shrimp stock—or the Brandied Shrimp Bisque recipe that's in this book.) If the whole shrimp aren't used right away, the heads will spoil quickly because of the fat. This is the primary reason for deheading shrimp before freezing. You can, however, make "spiders" from the heads by removing the carapace (the head part of the exoskeleton) from the cephalothorax (the underlying structure), like lifting the body on a funny car, dredging the exposed body and walking legs in batter, and then frying; I suppose this is like crustacean offal.

Who Knew That Something So Small Would Get So Big?

Those alien-looking marine creatures didn't look like food to many folks when Europeans first settled these parts and for some time afterward. Native Americans and early inhabitants were known to build weirs and other netlike devices to catch shrimp for subsistence—in other words, to keep from starving. Ports such as Galveston, New Orleans, Mobile, and St. Augustine, established by the French and Iberians, in whose culinary traditions shrimp were a prized delicacy, were the first to see a commercial shrimp harvest in the southeastern part of the country.

While in the eighteenth and nineteenth centuries fishermen in California dominated the shrimp catch, the shrimping industry would be centered in the South by 1908. It wasn't until after World War I that commercial harvesting of shrimp took off in the Carolinas. Trawlers followed the shrimp up the coast from Florida and Georgia, but Tar Heels were reluctant to adapt to this new commercial crop because they viewed shrimp as pests that fouled their fishing nets. These pests were traded inland for barrels of corn to farmers who would plow them under as fertilizer. Elizabeth Wiegand, author of *The Outer Banks Cookbook*, loves to relate stories of old-timers who still won't eat the pesky bugs.

The technological innovation that changed the shrimping industry by making large-scale harvesting possible was the otter trawl. After first appearing in Florida around 1913 and then being nearly universally used in the Carolinas by the Great Depression, this fishing gear required less labor, could operate in shallow water, and produced a greater effort-to-yield ratio than the purse seines that preceded it. The design of the otter trawl (as described above) is virtually the same today, except for the addition of the turtle exclusion device, which helps to eliminate inadvertent trapping and killing of marine turtles. With the increased size of annual harvests and identification of northern cities as markets for shrimp, canneries were opened along the Atlantic and Gulf coasts to dehead shrimp and preserve them for transport inland and north. By the 1940s, canning was in turn replaced with freezing, and even today, most shrimp are transported frozen.

It's hard to imagine now, but for a long time—even through the 1970s—shrimp remained a primarily regional, seasonal specialty. To enjoy shrimp at their most glorious freshness, a journey to coastal communities was necessary, and the cuisines of New Orleans and Charleston are prime examples of how shrimp cookery evolved due to the cities' proximity to prime shrimp habitats. By the 1980s, the science of successfully farming shrimp caught up to the desire of marketers to find the next big, cheap fast food to compete with chicken nuggets, and popcorn shrimp was born. This would propel shrimp to previously unimagined heights of popularity. In 2001, shrimp became the most popular seafood in the United States when sales surpassed those of canned tuna. And today, although shrimp range as far north as Long Island, North Carolina is the northernmost Atlantic shrimp fishery.

Now What?

It's difficult to overstate the importance of buying wild-caught American shrimp and the resulting impact of this on a unique segment of life in the South. Although the shrimping industry, per se, is relatively new, plying the waterways to catch food is a centuries-old profession along the Atlantic and Gulf coasts. That hardscrabble, salt-of-the-earth way of life is threatened by imported, farm-raised shrimp. Shrimp are one of the last truly wild creatures that we consume in significant quantities. By conscientiously sourcing our shrimp for the dinner table and understanding the history and culture of the people who harvest them, we can ensure that future generations will be able to consume shrimp as well. Anyone endowed with an excellent set of taste buds can tell the difference between free-range Atlantic or Gulf shrimp and those of dubious origin, but for the rest of us, it's imperative to ask questions and read labels. Although our food system is vibrant and dynamic and the proliferation of high-quality food purveyors makes responsible purchasing more realistic, it is often a challenge for even the most educated consumers to buy shrimp responsibly. Because of all of the options to choose from and all of the information to sift through, it's not easy to know what you're truly purchasing.

Culinary Renaissance

In the 1980s and 1990s, celebrity status was bestowed on those in the culinary profession and obscure ingredients from exotic locales were fetishized, but it was a dark period for recognizing our own locally sourced, high-quality ingredients. With the contemporary focus on wanting to know more about where our food comes from, wild-caught American shrimp have become beneficiaries of our increased awareness. The highest-quality ingredients don't have to be flown in from across the ocean; they're swimming right outside our back doors. At a time when large-species fisheries are being decimated by overharvesting, the American shrimp fishery is being recognized as one of the most viable sustainable fisheries in this country. Chefs are having a field day showcasing this bounty of southern waters in myriad ways, from the lobster roll–inspired Gulf Shrimp Rolls in this cookbook to traditional Thai Tom Yum Goong, from Shrimp and Leek Quiche to Shrimp Ceviche, from Shrimp and Spinach Enchiladas to Jambalaya.

You get what you pay for. Buying wild-caught American shrimp is the best choice for all concerned. According to the Monterey Bay Aquarium, a leading authority on sustainable fisheries and seafood conservation, "Most imported farmed shrimp should be avoided due to habitat damage, the risk of pollution and the introduction of non-native species to the surrounding environment." Just like anything else, farmed shrimp are a product of their environment, and if that environment is a closed system filled with agricultural runoff and effluent, the resultant shrimp are less pristine than those reared in the open seas.

Remember the impact of your decisions; you inform the world about what's important to you every time you spend money. That principle applies to everything from iPhones to charities, from automobiles to food. When you're drawing up your shopping list or cruising down an aisle at the supermarket, consider what types of items you would like to see more of and buy those. Are they made in a factory or grown on the land or in the sea? Consider the statement you would like to make about our food system, and purchase accordingly. The next time you're down at the coast, smell the briny air, seek out what's fresh on the docks, and commune with your ancestors. Do your part to help ensure that there always will be folks out on the salt.

The Nitty-Gritty Guide to Prepping Shrimp

THERE'S NO SHAME IN USING FROZEN SHRIMP

Unless you live on the coast or have direct access to shrimp boats, properly handled frozen shrimp are usually superior to "fresh" shrimp, primarily because of the speed at which the flesh breaks down. Shrimp are often frozen on the boat or at the dock and are preserved in a closer-to-fresh state than shrimp packed on ice and shipped or trucked to where you are. Remember, cold temperatures slow the decomposition of protein—the colder, the slower— but nothing prevents it.

Plan ahead; when done properly, this takes time. Thaw a frozen bag of shrimp in the refrigerator in a pan since water will probably leak out as it thaws. Invariably, at some point in its suspended animation (like Han Solo in carbonite), that bag has been bumped, jostled, or otherwise compromised. Freezing the shrimp in a block of ice helps maintain the integrity of the shrimp by providing an additional layer of protection for the shrimp. Some folks prefer using two layers of bags when freezing shrimp, assuming one will leak.

After about twenty-four hours, when the shrimp are mostly thawed, you'll see loose shrimp beginning to separate from each other inside the block of ice. Transfer the pan to your sink and commence peeling. A trickle of cold running water will finish the job of thawing the shrimp at the center of the block and will rinse your fingers periodically.

I'm right-handed, so lefties, bear with me and do the opposite. Hold the shrimp in your right hand, tail pointing right and down. Place your left thumb over the legs extending from the first two shell sections and unwrap the other side of the shell over the top of the tail and toward you. It should come off in one piece, maybe not the first time, but practice makes perfect and you'll get lots of practice. Transfer the shrimp to your left hand, without changing its orientation, tail still pointing right and down. Using your right thumb and index finger, squeeze the extreme end of the meat (where the last tail section connects to the fins) while pulling the meat with your left hand and removing the exoskeleton with your right.

Decide whether to devein the shrimp. This is determined by the company you keep and how fancy you are. Remember that "vein" is a euphemism because we're talking about a long, lean intestine filled with what intestines are normally filled with. Unless you have the most sensitive taste buds on the planet, it's only something you see, not something you taste. In South Louisiana, shrimp are deveined when necessary, usually when they're really big, really dirty, or destined for tourists. In North Carolina, folks look at you like you're uncivilized if the shrimp aren't deveined. When in Rome, eh? Others can debate the pros and cons, but I believe that when you buy wild-caught shrimp, they're cleaner and don't require deveining. If you would like to devein your shrimp, simply grasp the peeled shrimp in your left hand, tail pointing right and down, and use a sharp paring knife to make a ¼-inch-deep incision along the length of where the shrimp's backbone would be. Remove the vein, discard said digestive system, then submerge the shrimp in cool water to rinse.

Begin preparing your chosen recipe.

HOW DO YOU KNOW WHAT SIZE TO BUY?

There's no wrong answer to the question of what size shrimp to buy; the goal is to get the biggest bang for your buck. Use the smallest shrimp when making stuffing and salads or for recipes that call for chopping or puréeing. Medium shrimp are great for including in pastas and stews or when shrimp are a significant part of the whole. The largest shrimp are reserved for recipes that allow them to stand alone, where they'll be the focal point.

Shrimp are sold by size, so the numbers (U15, 21/25, 61/70) that you usually find accompanying shrimp in the marketplace are used to indicate how many shrimp of that size will be in a pound. U15 means there are under 15 shrimp per pound, and 21/25 means there are 21–25 shrimp per pound; therefore U15 shrimp are about twice the size of 21/25 shrimp, which are about twice the size of 41/50 shrimp. In general, when a recipe calls for jumbo shrimp, use U15 or 16/20; for large shrimp, use 21/25 or 26/30; for medium shrimp, use 31/40 or 41/50; and for small shrimp, use 61/70 or 71/90. Most folk find smaller, younger shrimp to be sweeter, which seems to be the rule for most proteins. The smaller the shrimp, the more likely you are to find them peeled. Be aware that buying peeled shrimp usually means that they contain higher levels of preservatives (used to retain water that's normally lost in freezing/thawing) and that they're more likely to be imported. Peeling shrimp is primarily done by hand, and if those hands are in the United States, the corresponding price of the shrimp goes up.

QUALITY IDENTIFIERS

When you buy shrimp at the dock or from a shrimper, the heads should still be attached. Remember that the joint where the headpiece abuts the first tail segment of the exoskeleton is where most of the animal's fat is stored. One great way to tell how fresh shrimp are is to determine whether that fat has begun to turn black, which happens about two to three days after the head-on shrimp have been out of the water, even under refrigeration. When buying headless shrimp, it's difficult to tell how fresh the shrimp are or if they've been previously frozen; that's why it's important to know the integrity of sellers and how quickly they turn over their inventory. (My father claims that shrimp are fresh if the whiskers aren't broken, but unfortunately most folks don't know that the shrimp they're buying are missing heads, much less that they should have whiskers.)

If you find yourself with a large quantity of fresh shrimp, sort the shrimp according to size: small, medium, large. Sizing shrimp helps ensure that they'll all be cooked to the same degree of doneness, instead of overcooking smaller shrimp and undercooking larger shrimp. Leave the heads on some to cook for dinner; pop off the heads of those that you plan to freeze. To freeze shrimp, fill resealable quart bags about three-quarters full with shrimp, then add filtered tap water to cover the shrimp. Squeeze the air out of the bags and seal. Write the size and date on the bags and lay them flat in the freezer. After the bags are frozen, they can be stacked or stood on end. Try to cook and eat frozen shrimp within six months.

Pairing with Beverages

Nothing heightens the experience of a meal like a well-conceived food-and-beverage pairing. The key to pairing beverages with different dishes is deciding which ingredients are most pronounced. The goal is to achieve balance both on the plate and between the food and the beverage. Remember that shrimp are essentially neutral, acidity balances fat, sweetness balances bitterness, and bitterness tempers spiciness. Not all of these attributes are present in every dish. Choosing the correct pairing often involves identifying what the recipe is lacking or has in abundance and balancing it with the drink. A well-balanced dish can usually be enjoyed with just about any beverage.

Remember that the dish can be adjusted up until the last minute, but the beverage is what it is. More or less acidity or fat/richness can be added to the dish just prior to serving. You can't take the same liberties with wine or beer, so success is in the choosing, the tasting, and the research.

When pairing any dish with wine, keep in mind which ingredients are deal breakers for particular wines, such as artichokes or asparagus, excess spiciness or acidity. Another key is to pair the dish with the wine you use in cooking it. You know a wine will complement a dish if it's included in the recipe. Often shrimp recipes, in this book or otherwise, call for a dry white wine (if you don't have dry white wine on hand, dry vermouth makes an excellent substitute). Sancerre, New Zealand Sauvignon Blanc, Chablis (the real French wine, not the California version that borrows the moniker), and Vouvray are wonderful with poached, grilled, and fried shrimp recipes. Pinot Noir and Côte Rôti may be red wines, but they're still potentially wonderful pairings for heartier shrimp dishes. Remember: seek out true-to-style wines, drink what you like, spend what you're comfortable spending, and keep an open mind.

With beer, the key is to either match or contrast the flavors of the dish with the drink. Beer is much easier to pair with food because of its effervescence and range of flavors. Hoppy beers go with spicier dishes like jambalaya or country captain; crisp lagers find harmony with boiled, poached, or garlicky shrimp that are unencumbered by a sauce; wheat beers are wonderful with salads; and porters and brown ales delightfully bring out the nuance in southern Louisiana classics like gumbo and étouffée.

Cocktails are more problematic with lighter dishes, as shrimp recipes tend to be. Just keep in mind that acidity in the glass can balance richness on the plate. Bitters or amaros, when used in a cocktail, can temper the spiciness of a dish in the same way that hops in an India pale ale can, like enjoying a sazerac with a spicy bowl of étouffée or gumbo. Lemons are often served with seafood to help awaken taste buds and heighten the flavors of subtle ingredients. Citrus in a cocktail can serve the same purpose, as long as the accompanying alcohol level doesn't numb the palate, just as a mimosa is a great accompaniment for a shrimp omelette or quiche. Don't forget about cultural connections as well; who could pass up having a margarita with shrimp tacos or enchiladas?

As nonalcoholic beverages go, lemonade has a place at the table because of shrimp's affinity for lemons. Not-too-sweet tea just might be the be-all and end-all.

In the following pages, you'll find classic recipes from the southern canon, home-style favorites, international renditions, and inspired creations. Unless otherwise noted in the recipes, the shrimp should be deheaded. Keep in mind that there's no wrong way to cook shrimp. These recipes are merely suggestions, and there are as many recipes for gumbo, jambalaya, tom yum goong, and étouffée as there are grandmothers in the world.

Small Plates

Cookbooks, like meals, must start somewhere. The beginning should set the tone for what's to follow. The recipes in this section can be served as hors d'oeuvres, appetizers, entrées, or even potluck contributions. Ultimately, I hope this book will help you realize that shrimp aren't just for special occasions. With a little preparation, there's a shrimp dish for every meal and every circumstance.

Bacon-Wrapped Shrimp Brochettes with Rhubarbecue Sauce

This recipe is a great use for the largest shrimp you can find. Everyone loves bacon and Pepper Jack cheese, but few can put their finger on the secret ingredient in the sauce for these brochettes. Rhubarb is a vegetable high in oxalic acid that's commonly used to provide tartness to sweet desserts. Here we play up the tangy fruitiness in what looks like an eastern North Carolina barbecue sauce, but the fine folks from Down East wouldn't claim it because of the sugar. The sweet tartness of the sauce cuts the richness of the bacon and cheese nicely.

MAKES 4–6 SERVINGS

FOR THE RHUBARBECUE SAUCE

(MAKES ABOUT 3 CUPS)

1¼ pounds rhubarb, chopped

1½ cups apple cider vinegar

½ cup water

2½ cups brown sugar

1 teaspoon allspice

½ teaspoon dry mustard

Pinch of cayenne pepper (or to taste)

FOR THE BROCHETTES

2 pounds jumbo shrimp (U15), peeled, head-on, with tails left on

Up to 30 slices high-quality, thick-sliced applewood-smoked bacon

Kosher salt and freshly ground black pepper

½ pound Pepper Jack cheese, grated

Bamboo skewers soaked in water

To make the Rhubarbecue Sauce, combine all ingredients in a saucepan, bring to a simmer, and cook for 15 minutes until the rhubarb is completely soft. Purée with an immersion blender, force through a strainer, and return the liquid to the saucepan. Reduce the sauce over low heat until it coats the back of a spoon.

To make the brochettes, preheat the oven to 300°. Devein the shrimp, slicing about halfway through the shrimp down the length of the back to make a pocket for the cheese.

Place the bacon in 1 or 2 layers on a baking sheet and bake for 5 minutes. The bacon should only be slightly rendered, not fully cooked. Remove from the oven and allow it to cool to the touch, leaving the rendered bacon fat in the baking sheet. Increase the oven temperature to 350°.

Sprinkle salt and pepper on the shrimp. Divide the grated cheese evenly between the shrimp, stuffing it into the incision. Using 1 piece of bacon per shrimp, starting at the head, wrap the bacon around the shrimp like a mummy, keeping the shrimp as straight as possible. Place each shrimp on a bamboo skewer, securing both ends of the bacon. When all of the shrimp have been prepared, transfer them to the baking sheet with the reserved bacon fat. Bake for 12 minutes, or until the cheese begins to ooze from the centermost shrimp. Using a slotted spatula, transfer the shrimp to a serving plate and drizzle with Rhubarbecue Sauce.

Salt-and-Pepper Shrimp

This recipe comes from the wonderful Andrea Reusing, a comrade-in-arms I have come to know through her involvement in various food-focused charity events. Her book, Cooking in the Moment, *definitely had an influence on me, and she is a role model of sustainable local sourcing. Lantern, her restaurant in Chapel Hill, North Carolina, puts a pan-Asian spin on the southern larder, such as this take on fried shrimp.*

MAKES 6 SERVINGS

1½ pounds medium shrimp (31/40), unpeeled
3 quarts vegetable oil
3 tablespoons plus 1 teaspoon kosher salt, divided
2 large egg whites, at room temperature
1 cup cornstarch
3 tablespoons plus 1 teaspoon freshly ground black
    pepper, divided
2 cups jalapeños, sliced ⅛ inch thick (about 8 jalapeños)
3 cups cilantro sprigs (from about 2 bunches)
2 teaspoons flaky sea salt, such as Maldon

Cut the shell along the back of each shrimp with small kitchen shears (don't peel), devein the shrimp, and snip off the legs.

Heat the oil to 400° in a heavy 8- to 10-quart pot.

Toss the shrimp with 1 tablespoon kosher salt and let stand for 5 minutes. Rinse under cold water, drain, and pat dry. Pulse the egg whites in a blender until watery, then transfer them to a bowl. In another bowl, stir together the cornstarch, 3 tablespoons pepper, and 2 tablespoons kosher salt.

Toss half of the shrimp with ½ teaspoon each of kosher salt and pepper in a third bowl. Dip them in the egg white, letting the excess drip off, then lightly dredge them in the cornstarch mixture, shaking off the excess. The coating should be as light as possible. Fry until they're crisp and cooked through, 1½–2 minutes. Using a slotted spoon, transfer the shrimp to paper towels to drain. Repeat with the remaining shrimp. Keep the shrimp in a warm oven.

Reduce the oil temperature to 375°.

Place half of the jalapeños in the oil, wait 10 seconds, then add half of the cilantro. After about 30 seconds, when the cilantro just starts to turn dark green and the jalapeños are wilted, transfer them with a slotted spoon to paper towels to drain. Don't let the jalapeños or cilantro get brown. The cilantro will crisp as it cools. Repeat with the remaining jalapeños and cilantro.

Arrange the shrimp on a platter, scatter the jalapeños and cilantro over the top, and season with the sea salt.

Shrimp and Leek Quiche

My first encounter with quiche was as a tween trying out recipes from the cookbook that came with our newfangled microwave. Quiche Lorraine was my favorite recipe from that book, but to this day, I'm baffled by cooking eggs in a microwave. Regardless, I love a nice slice of quiche for a late Sunday breakfast or a light summer lunch. Remember to wash the leeks well after cutting—they're notorious for harboring sand and soil. Also, save the green tops for use when making stock or preparing a Low Country boil.

MAKES 4–6 SERVINGS

2 tablespoons unsalted butter

½ cup julienned leeks

½ pound small shrimp (71/90), peeled, or leftover large boiled shrimp, peeled and chopped

½ tablespoon minced garlic

½ teaspoon kosher salt

¼ teaspoon white pepper

¼ pound spinach, julienned

1½ tablespoons all-purpose flour

1 cup grated sharp white cheddar cheese

3 large eggs

½ cup half-and-half

Pinch of nutmeg

1 unbaked pie shell

Preheat the oven to 350°.

Melt the butter in a sauté pan over medium-low heat and sweat the leeks until they're tender, about 10 minutes. Increase the heat to medium, add the shrimp and garlic, and season with the salt and white pepper; cook for 3 minutes, or until the shrimp are mostly done. Add the spinach and cook until wilted. Remove the pan from the heat, stir in the flour until combined, and add the cheese. Allow to cool a bit.

In a bowl, whisk together the eggs, half-and-half, and nutmeg, then stir in the cooled shrimp mixture. Pour the egg mixture into the pie shell. Bake for 35 minutes, or until a knife inserted in the center comes out clean. Cool on a wire rack for 15 minutes or so, then cut into wedges and serve.

Bertie County Company Shrimp and Crackers

This recipe comes from Carroll Leggett, a native of Bertie County, North Carolina, who has led many lives and is acquainted with just about everyone in the state who knows what unbolted cornmeal is. He is a wonderfully entertaining writer, a bon vivant, and a dear friend. This is a dish handed down from his grandmother, Nonie Stella Harden (née Castellow), who ran a boardinghouse and owned and operated the Busy Bee Café in Windsor, North Carolina, from the 1920s to the 1940s. Carroll says, "A tiny bit of heat added (Texas Pete, Tabasco) would be okay, but I'm cautious about doing that for a general audience. Lots of diners don't appreciate surprise heat. And Texas Pete will alter the flavor. You may want to reserve a couple of whole shrimp for garnish with cilantro."

MAKES 8 SERVINGS AS A STARTER

---

1 pound small-to-medium shrimp (61/70 or 41/50), peeled and deveined

3 tablespoons cream cheese, at room temperature

2 tablespoons sweet pickle juice

2 tablespoons finely diced spring onions (or green onions)

4 tablespoons finely chopped sweet pickles

3 tablespoons finely chopped red bell peppers

1 cup finely chopped celery

3 tablespoons chopped cilantro

1 teaspoon sea salt

1/4 teaspoon freshly ground black pepper

2 teaspoons Grey Poupon mustard

1/4 cup Duke's mayonnaise

Saltine crackers

Cook the shrimp in salted water. Bring the water to a boil, simmer 3–4 minutes, remove the shrimp, place in ice water, and drain, patting them dry with paper towels.

Place the shrimp, cream cheese, and pickle juice in a food processor and pulse until the shrimp are finely minced and blended. Remove to a bowl. Add the spring onions, sweet pickles, red bell peppers, celery, cilantro, sea salt, and pepper and mix. Add the mustard and mayonnaise and mix thoroughly. If necessary, add additional mayonnaise to get the desired consistency. Serve with crackers.

Shrimp with Cocktail Sauce

At one point in our nation's history, shrimp cocktail was a dish that symbolized luxury. That era has gone the way of the passenger pigeon, and now bottled cocktail sauces are available just about anywhere. Countless pale imitations don't lessen the experience of pristine jumbo shrimp cooked well and dipped in a delightfully tangy sauce. Feel free to adapt the sauce recipe to your liking.

MAKES 4 SERVINGS

FOR THE COCKTAIL SAUCE

¼ cup prepared horseradish
1 cup Heinz ketchup
¼ cup Crystal hot sauce
2 teaspoons lemon juice
2 teaspoons Lea & Perrins Worcestershire sauce

FOR THE SHRIMP

1 gallon water
⅓ cup kosher salt
2 lemons, cut in half
3 ribs celery, chopped
½ large yellow onion, sliced
4 bay leaves
¼ cup red chili flakes
2 pounds jumbo shrimp (U15), peeled
Celery leaves

To make the sauce, whisk together all ingredients in a bowl.

To make the shrimp, combine all ingredients except the shrimp in a stockpot and bring to a boil. Cook for 10 minutes. Add the shrimp And return to a boil. Cook for 1 minute, then remove from the heat and allow to sit for 5 minutes before removing the shrimp. Cool.

Serve the shrimp on a platter, artfully arranged with celery leaves and a bowl of cocktail sauce. Or make individual servings by placing equal amounts of cocktail sauce in the bottom of 4 martini glasses and hooking the shrimp around the rim of each glass.

Saucy Cocktail with Shrimp

Waiting for a table at Jacques Imo's restaurant in New Orleans, my wife ordered a bloody mary, and it had every conceivable garnish you could think of, including a boiled head-on shrimp. Genius! I like to incorporate Cackalacky Spice Sauce (a sweet potato–based hot sauce from Chapel Hill, North Carolina) into my bloody marys. If you can't find Cackalacky sauce in your neck of the woods, you can get oomph from the pepper sauce of your choosing. Maybe we can call this the W. C. Fields shrimp cocktail?

In South Louisiana, everyone's pantry contains that familiar green can of Creole seasoning. If that's your tradition, feel free to use it in the following recipes that call for such. If you don't have Creole seasoning in your cabinet, I've included a simple recipe that can be made in even larger batches and stored in a Mason jar or other resealable container.

MAKES 1 DRINK

FOR THE CREOLE SEASONING
(MAKES ABOUT ³⁄₄ CUP)

3 tablespoons paprika
1¹⁄₂ tablespoons kosher salt
¹⁄₂ tablespoon celery salt
2 tablespoons granulated garlic
1 tablespoon freshly ground black pepper
1 tablespoon granulated onion
1 tablespoon cayenne pepper
2 teaspoons ground oregano
2 teaspoons ground thyme

FOR THE BLOODY MARY MIX
(MAKES ENOUGH FOR ABOUT 12 DRINKS)

1 (46-ounce) can of V8 juice
¹⁄₄ cup lime juice
6 tablespoons Lea & Perrins Worcestershire sauce

2 tablespoons Sambal Oelek Chili Paste
6 tablespoons Cackalacky Spice Sauce
1 teaspoon celery salt
2 teaspoons freshly ground black pepper
1 teaspoon kosher salt
1 tablespoon mustard seeds, cracked
¼ cup tomato paste
1 teaspoon granulated onion
1 teaspoon granulated garlic

FOR THE DRINK
1 lime wedge
2 teaspoons Creole seasoning
Ice
2 ounces citrusy gin (like TOPO Piedmont Gin from
   Chapel Hill, North Carolina)
4 ounces bloody mary mix
Pickled okra
Boiled shrimp

To make the Creole seasoning, add all ingredients to an airtight container and shake well to evenly distribute.

To make the bloody mary mix, combine all ingredients in a bowl and whisk until well blended. Store in the refrigerator in a nonreactive container for up to 2 weeks.

To make the drink, rub the lime wedge around the rim of a pint glass. Sprinkle the Creole seasoning on a saucer and dip the rim of the glass in the seasoning. Fill the glass with ice. Add the gin, then the bloody mary mix, and stir with a chopstick. Add the lime wedge and as much pickled okra and boiled shrimp as you would like to munch on while you sip your cocktail.

Shrimp Ceviche

I'm a big fan of Latin flavors, and you'll often find me cooking or eating something in this culinary vein on my days off from the restaurant. Remember, the difference between a tartare and a ceviche is that a tartare is raw, a ceviche is not—the protein is denatured by acid instead of heat, indicated by a change of texture in the protein. The amount of time needed for the protein to be "cooked" by the acid depends on the thickness of the shrimp, so we cut them in half. Mild white seafood like sea scallops or grouper works well as a substitute. This recipe was developed for an event with Brad Wynn of Big Boss Brewing in Raleigh, North Carolina, because he loves ceviche and it pairs wonderfully with his brewery's Angry Angel Kölsch Style Ale.

MAKES 4 SERVINGS AS AN APPETIZER

1 pound large shrimp (21/25), peeled
¼ cup seeded, small-diced Roma tomatoes
4 teaspoons seeded, minced jalapeños
1 cup lime juice
½ cup small-diced red onions
2 tablespoons packed cilantro
2 tablespoons orange juice
⅓ cup lemon juice
2 teaspoons kosher salt
Plantain crisps or tortilla chips
Hot sauce (preferably Valentina or Bufalo)

Cut the shrimp in half lengthwise. Place in a bowl and cover with water. Swish around well, then remove the shrimp from the water. Combine the shrimp with the remaining ingredients in a shallow pan or bowl. Cover with plastic wrap and press it down onto the surface of the ceviche. Refrigerate for at least 4 hours or overnight, stirring halfway through and replacing the plastic wrap.

To serve, use a slotted spoon to transfer the ceviche to a serving dish. Serve with plantain crisps or tortilla chips and a bottle of hot sauce. Some folks like to serve the juice separately as shots of "Leche de Tigre."

Shrimp Aspic

In the 1970s, I always wondered what those copper molds hanging in relatives' houses were for—obviously not gelatin desserts, which were served in special Tupperware containers. Aspics, like shrimp or tomato aspic, are holdovers from the age of beehive hairdos and beyond, when it was in vogue to bring gelatin-enhanced savory dishes to large gatherings. There's plenty of flavor here, and I recommend saltine crackers for serving (or Ritz if you're fancy). I first served this at the inaugural Green Acres Gala Fundraiser for the Edible Schoolyard at the Greensboro Children's Museum in North Carolina.

MAKES 4 CUPS

½ pound small shrimp (71/90), peeled
1 teaspoon Creole seasoning (page 26)
1 cup chopped celery
¾ cup chopped yellow onions
1½ cups V8 juice
1½ teaspoons minced dill
1½ tablespoons unflavored gelatin, dissolved according to package directions
½ pound cream cheese, at room temperature
1 cup mayonnaise
1 tablespoon lemon juice
½ teaspoon kosher salt
½ teaspoon freshly ground black pepper

Season the shrimp with the Creole seasoning and sauté in a small skillet until cooked. Allow to cool. Place the celery, onions, and shrimp in a food processor and purée. Squeeze the liquid from the puréed mixture. Heat the V8 juice gently in a small saucepan and stir in the dill and gelatin. Place the cream cheese in the bowl of a stand mixer with the paddle attachment and mix until smooth. Add the puréed mixture and mayonnaise and mix well. Add the remaining ingredients and mix well. Turn the mixture into a decorative mold and chill until set. Unmold to serve.

NOTE ❋ It isn't cheating to line the mold with plastic wrap to facilitate removal of the aspic, but be prepared to lose some of the definition of the mold design.

Shrimp Omelet

Often the best breakfast dishes are those that deliver the greatest flavor for the least effort—this is one of those dishes. Easily made with leftover cooked shrimp and roasted peppers from a jar, it can be sexed up with home-roasted peppers (red or poblano) and the addition of crabmeat or bay scallops. Baby spinach is another wonderful option that adds volume and mineral complexity to the omelet. If you find yourself reaching for a glass of Grüner Veltliner to go with this omelet, that's how breakfast becomes brunch.

MAKES 1 SERVING

2 tablespoons canola oil

3 ounces small shrimp (71/90), boiled and peeled,
 or leftover large boiled shrimp, peeled and chopped

¼ cup julienned roasted red peppers

2 pinches kosher salt

Pinch of freshly ground black pepper

3 large eggs, beaten

2 ounces goat cheese, crumbled

2 tablespoons chopped green onions

Heat the oil in a nonstick skillet over medium-low heat. Add the shrimp and red peppers and heat through; season with the salt and pepper. Pour the eggs over the shrimp mixture; shake the pan and lift the edges of the eggs with a rubber spatula to allow the liquid to run underneath. When the eggs are mostly set but still a little runny on top, sprinkle the goat cheese and green onions on to the center third of the omelet. Fold the omelet in thirds, like folding a letter, and turn out onto a plate.

Prized Pickled Shrimp

Down South, many families have a favorite recipe for pickled shrimp, which surely originated as a preservation technique but soon developed into a cocktail party staple. This version comes from Marleah Hobbs, a retired art professor and mother of the iconic southern artist Blair Hobbs. She writes, "I don't remember when or where I first saw this recipe, but it was a favorite party dish in Oxford and, for the last thirty-five years, in Auburn."

MAKES 8 SERVINGS AS A STARTER

FOR THE MARINADE
1¼ cups canola oil
¾ cup white wine vinegar
2½ tablespoons capers and their brine
2½ teaspoons celery seeds
1½ teaspoons sea salt
Dash of Tabasco sauce

FOR THE SHRIMP
½ cup celery tops
¼ cup pickling spice
3½ teaspoons sea salt
2½ pounds large shrimp (21/25), unpeeled
2 cups thinly sliced yellow onions
8 bay leaves

To make the marinade, mix all ingredients well in a bowl.

To make the shrimp, in a stockpot, bring 6 quarts water to a boil. Add the celery tops, pickling spice, and salt; return the water to a boil and add the shrimp. Boil until the shrimp turn pink. Drain, then submerge in cold water. Peel and devein the shrimp.

In a shallow dish, alternate the shrimp with the onions and bay leaves. Cover with the marinade and chill for at least 24 hours, stirring occasionally. Serve within a week.

Coconut Fried Shrimp with Mango-Teriyaki Sauce

The Polynesian flair of this dish hearkens back to Trader Vic's and the heyday of pupu platters. Lately, there has been a resurgence in quasi-tropical combinations, of which this may be the ultimate. This is amazing if you can get shrimp with heads on, but don't fret if you can only find headless. Because of the variation in the size of shrimp, you may need to make more of the wet or dry mix for the breading. Scale up as necessary. The sauce might be better if you substitute ripe peaches for the mangoes.

MAKES 4–6 SERVINGS

FOR THE MANGO-TERIYAKI SAUCE
(MAKES ABOUT 2 CUPS)
2-inch piece of ginger, peeled and thinly sliced
1 cup unsweetened pineapple juice
$\frac{1}{2}$ cup dark brown sugar
$\frac{1}{2}$ cup Japanese soy sauce (not low-sodium)
$\frac{1}{4}$ cup chopped green onions
1 pound mangoes (about 2 large mangoes),
    peeled and chopped

FOR THE SHRIMP
2 pounds jumbo shrimp (16/20), unpeeled,
    with or without heads
1 cup all-purpose flour
1 large egg, beaten
1 cup unsweetened coconut milk
1 cup whole milk
1 teaspoon kosher salt, plus more for serving
1 cup panko breadcrumbs
1 cup unsweetened coconut flakes

To make the Mango-Teriyaki Sauce, combine all ingredients in a medium saucepan and bring to a simmer over medium heat. Cook until the mangoes are tender, 15–20 minutes. Purée with an immersion blender, strain through a sieve into a bowl, and discard the solids. The sauce should coat the back of a spoon. Cool.

To make the shrimp, heat oil in a deep fryer to 350°. If using head-on shrimp, only peel the middle segments of the shrimp, leaving the head and final tail segment attached. If using deheaded shrimp, peel while leaving the final tail segment attached.

Prepare three shallow pans for breading the shrimp. Place the flour in the first pan. In the second pan, combine the egg, coconut milk, milk, and salt. In the third pan, mix the bread-crumbs and coconut. Working with a few shrimp at a time, dust the shrimp in flour and shake off the excess before transferring them to the second pan with the egg mixture. Remember to keep one hand wet and one hand dry to avoid breading your fingers. Remove each shrimp from the egg mixture with a fork, allowing the excess egg to run off, then place it in the third pan with the breadcrumb mixture. Using your dry hand, cover the shrimp with coconut and breadcrumbs and press firmly so the breadcrumb mixture adheres to the shrimp. Transfer the breaded shrimp to a dry plate and repeat until all shrimp are breaded before you begin frying.

The shrimp should be fried in small batches until golden brown, 3–5 minutes. Transfer to a platter lined with paper towels and sprinkle with kosher salt. Allow to cool just a tad before serving. Serve with Mango-Teriyaki Sauce.

New Orleans–Style Barbecue Shrimp in South Carolina

Joe and Heidi Trull are from the Carolinas—he, North; she, South. We met in New Orleans, where Joe was a stellar pastry chef and Heidi ran a funky diner in the Bywater neighborhood. They have since relocated to Belton, South Carolina, where they own and operate Grits and Groceries and have become pillars of the community. Says Joe, "This is a play on the New Orleans dish of barbecue shrimp. I decided that we had to make it in a South Carolina style, so I started using my Carolina-inspired Beer-B-Que Sauce." His Louisiana Beer-B-Que Sauce and Low Country Seasoning are available online at www.gritsandgroceries.com. The recipe for the seasoning is included below, but if you can't get your hands on the sauce, he says you can substitute a sweet-and-tangy sauce, such as the original Bone Suckin' Sauce (but it won't be as good).

MAKES 8 SERVINGS

FOR THE LOW COUNTRY SEASONING
(MAKES 2½ CUPS)

½ cup kosher salt

½ cup celery salt

⅓ cup dry mustard

¼ cup minced garlic

¼ cup freshly ground black pepper

¼ cup white pepper

¼ cup cayenne pepper

2 tablespoons plus 1 teaspoon ground bay leaves

5 pounds jumbo shrimp (16/20), peeled
1 tablespoon Low Country Seasoning
1 cup Louisiana Beer-B-Que Sauce or other
    sweet-and-tangy barbecue sauce
2 sticks unsalted butter
4 cups white mushrooms, halved
1 can of beer, preferably malt liquor
¼ cup finely chopped parsley

To make the Low Country Seasoning, combine all ingredients in a bowl. Store in an airtight container.

Season the shrimp with the Low Country Seasoning. Combine the sauce and butter in a large sauté pan and cook over medium heat until the butter melts, stirring to combine. Add the shrimp, mushrooms, and beer, stir to combine, then cover. Cook until the shrimp are pink and firm, about 10 minutes. Serve garnished with the parsley over grits, rice, or mashed potatoes.

Salads

Boiled shrimp can be added to just about any salad, but in the following pages, you'll find some salads that are truly meal-worthy. Of course, each portion can be divided in half to make tantalizing starter salads.

Grilled Shrimp Caesar Salad

Ever since Paul Hogan threw shrimp on the barbie to promote Australian tourism, that backyard practice has taken off in the United States. Grilled shrimp is one of the easiest dishes to mess up. Keep in mind that shrimp are incredibly lean, so they're prone to drying out when cooked with dry heat. The keys here are the oil (which conducts the heat and causes the shrimp to cook faster) and the gaps between the shrimp on the skewer (a larger gap speeds up the cooking time since it allows the heat to get between the shrimp). The slam dunk would be peeling the shrimp while leaving the heads attached so the natural fat moistens the meat. For both the salad and the shrimp, more lemon is a good thing, so encourage diners to squeeze the lemon halves over their salads.

MAKES 4 SERVINGS

FOR THE DRESSING (MAKES ABOUT 1 QUART)

1 tablespoon minced garlic

1 large egg

½ cup lemon juice

1 tablespoon brown mustard (like Gulden's)

1 tablespoon Dijon mustard

¼ cup Lea & Perrins Worcestershire sauce

1 tablespoon kosher salt

1 teaspoon freshly ground black pepper

2 cups canola oil

1 cup extra-virgin olive oil

¼ pound Parmesan, grated

FOR THE SHRIMP

1 pound large shrimp (21/25), peeled and deveined

2 tablespoons canola oil

1 tablespoon kosher salt

2 teaspoons freshly ground black pepper

8 skewers

1 head romaine, quartered lengthwise
2 tablespoons canola oil
4 teaspoons kosher salt
2 teaspoons freshly ground black pepper
1 cup dressing
2 lemons, cut in half
Croutons

To make the dressing, add all but the last three ingredients to a blender and blend until smooth. Add the oils in a slow stream with the motor running. Transfer the dressing to a storage container and stir in the cheese until evenly distributed. The dressing can be stored in the refrigerator for up to 2 weeks.

To make the shrimp, mix the oil, salt, and pepper in a bowl, then toss the shrimp in the oil. Place the shrimp on the skewers, three to four shrimp each, leaving at least ½ inch between them. Grill the shrimp until opaque, but be careful not to dry them out.

To make the salad, brush the sides of the romaine wedges with the oil and sprinkle with the salt and pepper. Grill for 90 seconds on each side until lightly charred but not wilted. Remove the romaine to serving plates and ladle ¼ cup dressing over the romaine. Lay the shrimp over the dressing, two skewers to a plate in an "X" pattern. Place half a lemon at twelve o'clock and sprinkle with croutons.

Popcorn Shrimp Rémoulade Salad

Shrimp rémoulade salad is a traditional cold salad of iceberg lettuce, poached shrimp, and a zesty mayonnaise-based dressing. I thought we could turn that on its head and serve the ever-popular popcorn shrimp over a salad of crunchy romaine with classic house-salad accompaniments.

MAKES 4 SERVINGS

FOR THE RÉMOULADE (MAKES ABOUT 1 CUP)
1/4 cup mayonnaise
1/4 cup chowchow, drained
1/4 cup spicy brown mustard
1 tablespoon hot sauce (like Crystal or Texas Pete)

FOR THE SHRIMP
1 pound small shrimp (71/90), peeled
1/2 cup hot sauce (like Crystal or Texas Pete)
1 cup breading (page 64)
1 tablespoon Creole seasoning (page 26)

FOR THE SALAD
4 romaine hearts, chopped
3/4 cup rémoulade
1 cup peeled, seeded, diced cucumbers
4 hard-boiled eggs, diced
2 medium tomatoes, quartered
1 lemon, cut into eight wedges

To make the rémoulade, whisk together all ingredients in a bowl and chill.

To make the shrimp, heat oil in a deep fryer to 350°. In a bowl, marinate the shrimp in the hot sauce for 5–10 minutes. Place the breading in a shallow dish. Using a slotted spoon or your fingers, transfer the shrimp to the breading and toss to coat. Using a strainer, shake off the excess breading and fry the shrimp until they begin to float, 2–3 minutes. Remove the shrimp to a plate lined with paper towels. Sprinkle with the Creole seasoning.

To make the salad, in a bowl, toss together the romaine and rémoulade. Divide between 4 serving bowls and top with fried shrimp, cucumbers, eggs, 2 tomato wedges, and 2 lemon wedges.

Shrimp and Peach Salad

I originally created this salad with mangoes instead of peaches as a tropical, Caribbean-style summer salad. I changed the mangoes to peaches for a television cooking segment on peaches and was truly delighted by the marriage of flavors in the dish. Skeptics may read the list of ingredients and doubt it can be so tasty, but through the use of culinary algebra $(avocado + shrimp \times peach^{honey+lime}/ spinach)$, it all tastes great together.

MAKES 4 SERVINGS

---

1 tablespoon extra-virgin olive oil
$\frac{1}{2}$ teaspoon kosher salt
$\frac{1}{2}$ teaspoon freshly ground black pepper
$\frac{1}{2}$ pound baby spinach
$\frac{1}{4}$ cup lime juice
$\frac{1}{4}$ cup honey
3 peaches, peeled, pitted, and sliced
$\frac{3}{4}$ cup thinly sliced red onions
1 pound large shrimp (21/25), poached or steamed
    and peeled
1 avocado, sliced

Add the olive oil, salt, and pepper to a bowl and combine well. Toss the spinach in the oil mixture, then evenly divide it between 4 serving bowls. Add the lime juice and honey to the same bowl and combine well. Add the peaches, onions, and shrimp, tossing to coat. Arrange the peach mixture over the spinach in each bowl. Garnish the top of each salad with avocado slices.

Roasted Shrimp Salad

The beauty of this recipe is that it works with any kind of leftover cooked shrimp, but roasting the shrimp intensifies the flavor. This shrimp salad is wonderful on toast, on iceberg lettuce with cucumbers (and maybe some Thousand Island dressing), or as a tomato stuffing—just cut 4 tomatoes in half horizontally, squeeze out the seeds, season with salt and pepper, and top each half with a healthy dollop of this salad.

MAKES 4 SERVINGS

1 tablespoon canola oil
½ teaspoon smoked paprika
½ teaspoon granulated garlic
Pinch of cayenne pepper
¼ teaspoon freshly ground black pepper
2 teaspoons kosher salt, divided
1 pound small shrimp (61/70), peeled
½ cup minced red onions
¾ cup minced celery
¾ cup mayonnaise
3 dashes hot sauce (like Crystal or Texas Pete)
1 teaspoon lemon juice

Preheat the oven to 350°.

Add the oil to a bowl, mix in the smoked paprika, granulated garlic, cayenne pepper, and black pepper and 1 teaspoon of the salt, then add the shrimp and toss well to coat. Spread the shrimp in a single layer on a parchment-lined baking sheet. Bake for 5–7 minutes, just until the shrimp are opaque. Remove from the oven and allow the shrimp to cool.

In a bowl, combine the remaining ingredients. Fold in the shrimp.

Soups

In our home, we love to cook a big pot of soup for dinner on rainy days. These soups are even better the next day for lunch, either because the flavors have melded overnight or because the meal preparation involves only reheating for a few minutes. I generally don't use a recipe when making soup, preferring to use whatever ingredients I find in the fridge that play well together. For this collection, though, I enlisted some friends to share their favorite shrimp soup recipes. Nancie McDermott and Elizabeth Wiegand contributed truly transcendent preparations, and Beth Abadies's mirliton soup is full of the flavors of my youth.

Seafood Gumbo

There are three types of gumbo: Cajun, Creole, and something made in Charleston with tomatoes. My Granny Esma Trosclair, on my mother's side, always made a Creole-style chicken and sausage gumbo that was thickened with okra or filé (ground sassafras leaves) instead of a roux. My father's mother, Rena Clement, made a Cajun gumbo that was thickened with a roux. To each her own. This gumbo falls somewhere in the middle. I love a little of each, so I use okra and less roux than normal and I offer filé at the table. Remember—the darker the roux, the less thickening power it has. Seafood gumbo is almost always darker and thinner than other gumbos.

MAKES 8 SERVINGS

1 cup canola oil, divided
½ pound smoked pork sausage (I like kielbasa),
    cut in half lengthwise and sliced
1 cup all-purpose flour
1 large yellow onion, medium-diced
1 pound okra, sliced (thawed if frozen)
2 medium green bell peppers, medium-diced
4 ribs celery, medium-diced
2 tablespoons minced garlic
2 tablespoons Lea & Perrins Worcestershire sauce
2 tablespoons soy sauce or tamari
2 tablespoons Crystal hot sauce
1 gallon cold water
6 blue crabs (top shell, apron, and dead men removed),
    cleaned and cut in half
4 bay leaves
2 teaspoons thyme
1 tablespoon kosher salt
2 teaspoons freshly ground black pepper
½ teaspoon cayenne pepper
1 pint shucked oysters

1 pound medium shrimp (41/50), peeled
⅓ cup chopped Italian parsley
½ cup chopped green onions
Cooked long-grain rice

In a heavy-bottomed Dutch oven, heat 2 tablespoons of the oil over medium heat and add the sausage. When the sausage is browned on the edges and has given up some of its fat, remove to a plate.

Add the remaining oil to the pot over medium heat and when hot, stir in the flour with a wooden spoon. Continue stirring until the roux is the color of toasted pecans, or darker if you're brave. If the roux burns, discard it and start over. Be careful— the oil is about 400° and hot roux is very dangerous. When you achieve the darkest color you can, remove the pot from the heat and stir in the onion. Steam will erupt, so be careful. (This may sound overly detailed, but this is why gumbo-making skills evolve over time to become truly transcendent.)

Continue stirring off the heat as the onion sizzles, then add the okra and stir. Add the bell peppers, celery, and garlic And keep stirring. Add the Worcestershire sauce, soy sauce, and hot sauce; stir to combine. Now add the cold water, stirring constantly to avoid forming lumps. When all of the water has been incorporated, add the crabs.

Bring the liquid to a simmer, then add the bay leaves, thyme, salt, black pepper, cayenne pepper, and sausage and simmer for about 30 minutes. The broth should have thickened a little, the vegetables should be tender, and the whole house should smell like crab. Taste the broth for salt and pepper (you can always sneak in a little bit of Creole seasoning if you like). Add the oysters and shrimp and simmer just until they're done. Turn off the heat, remove the bay leaves, and stir in the parsley and green onions. Serve over rice.

Cream of Fennel Soup with Shrimp

Inspiration sometimes comes from unlikely sources. This soup was inspired by a cooking demonstration at the Crescent City Farmers Market in New Orleans that I attended as a young line cook around 2001. Anne Kearney, then chef/proprietor of the city's most well-regarded restaurant, Peristyle, made a mirliton slaw with tarragon dressing and poached gulf shrimp. It was a revelation on many levels, but I fell in love with the flavor of sweet shrimp accented by anise. This is my take on that combination of flavors.

MAKES 6–8 SERVINGS

1 stick unsalted butter

3 pounds fennel bulbs, thinly sliced

2 cups diced yellow onions

1 quart shrimp stock

1 quart chicken broth

2 teaspoons chopped garlic

½ tablespoon kosher salt

½ teaspoon white pepper

½ teaspoon basil

½ cup heavy cream

1 tablespoon anisette (like Ouzo or Sambucca)

1 tablespoon lemon juice

1 pound medium shrimp (31/40), peeled

Melt the butter in a saucepan over medium-low heat and sweat the fennel and onions until golden and soft, about 20 minutes. Add the shrimp stock, chicken broth, garlic, salt, white pepper, and basil; simmer for 5–10 minutes. Add the cream, anisette, and lemon juice and bring to a simmer. Cook for 5 minutes.

Purée with an immersion blender and strain through a medium-holed strainer. Return to the saucepan and add the shrimp. Simmer until the shrimp are opaque, taste for salt, and serve.

Mirliton and Shrimp Soup

The key ingredient in this soup is mirliton, a member of the cucurbit family and a bigger, lumpier cousin of the Mexican chayote squash. In South Louisiana, this subtle-tasting vegetable is used as a substitute for eggplant in many recipes. It wasn't uncommon, before Hurricane Katrina, for folks throughout New Orleans to have mirliton vines growing on their back fences. Being a culinary doppelganger, mirlitons can adapt to whatever ingredients you use with them. This recipe is from a friend, Beth Abadie, who loves having a good time, and this soup is definitely that.

MAKES 6–8 SERVINGS

6 medium mirlitons or chayote squashes
6 slices bacon, chopped
3 garlic cloves, minced
1 large green bell pepper, chopped
2 large white onions, chopped
4 shallots, chopped
2 tablespoons chopped flat-leaf parsley
1 teaspoon chopped tarragon
5 cups chicken stock
3 pounds small-to-medium shrimp (61/70 or 41/50),
    peeled and deveined
2 tablespoons unsalted butter
1 cup heavy cream
1 teaspoon cayenne pepper (or to taste)
Kosher salt and freshly ground black pepper, to taste

In a large pot, boil the mirlitons until tender. Cool, peel, core, and cut into cubes.

In a large pot, fry the bacon until golden brown and crisp. Add the garlic, green bell pepper, onions, shallots, parsley, and tarragon and sauté until slightly wilted and aromatic. Add the cubed mirlitons and chicken stock, then bring to a boil, reduce the heat, and simmer for 45 minutes to 1 hour. Remove the soup from the heat and let cool slightly.

While the soup is cooling, sauté the shrimp in the butter just until they turn pink. Purée the soup in batches in a blender or food processor until smooth. Return to a pot over low heat, add the cream, and stir until the cream is well incorporated. With a slotted spoon, add the shrimp to the soup, then add the cayenne pepper, salt, and black pepper and stir well. Heat through and serve.

Tom Yum Goong, a Thai Shrimp Soup

A dear friend and accomplished cookbook writer, Nancie McDermott fell in love with food all over again while in the Peace Corps in Thailand. I asked her for a definitive take on shrimp from that part of the world. She kindly obliged, saying, "Thais serve this classic, intensely flavored soup with lots of rice and an array of contrasting dishes. Preparing the ingredients takes a little time, while cooking takes a very few minutes. (Thais leave the lemongrass, galangal, and wild lime leaves in the soup. If you want to remove them, strain the hot soup into the serving bowl. Quickly scoop out the shrimp and mushrooms, add them to the soup, and serve.)"

MAKES 4–6 SERVINGS

3 tablespoons lime juice

2 tablespoons Asian fish sauce (nuoc mam)

1 tablespoon roasted chili paste (nahmprikpao)

5 small green and red Thai chilies

About ¼ cup cilantro leaves, torn or very coarsely chopped

3 stalks lemongrass

3 large, thin slices galangal

10 wild lime leaves

4 cups chicken or shrimp stock

¾ cup thinly sliced shiitake mushroom caps or small
   button mushrooms

½ pound large shrimp (26/30), peeled and deveined,
   tails left on

In a 1½-quart serving bowl, combine the lime juice, fish sauce, and roasted chili paste. Place the Thai chilies on a cutting board and press down on each one with the side of a cleaver or chef's knife to bruise it and release a little heat. Add the chilies to the serving bowl. Place the bowl by the stove, with the cilantro leaves on the side.

To prepare the lemongrass, trim each stalk down to about 5 inches, including the bulb-shaped base. Cut off the roots, leaving a smooth base. Discard the tops, roots, and any dried, outer leaves. Slice the stalks diagonally to make thin ovals, exposing as much of the interior of the stalk as possible. Place the lemongrass slices in a 2-quart saucepan along with the galangal slices. Tear the lime leaves in half (or quarter them if they're large). Place half of the lime leaves in the serving bowl and half in the saucepan.

Add the chicken or shrimp stock to the saucepan over medium-high heat and bring it to a lively boil. As soon as it boils, reduce the heat to maintain a gentle but lively simmer.

Add the mushrooms. Cook for 1 minute, stirring often. Add the shrimp and cook just until they become firm and pink, about 2 minutes more. Remove from the heat and pour the soup into the serving bowl. Stir well to mix the seasonings into the soup. Scatter the cilantro leaves over the soup and serve hot.

Rosemary Shrimp and
White Bean Soup

I grew up eating navy beans, but when I discovered cannellinis, there was no looking back—they just may be the perfect bean. I love white beans and shrimp in a soup or in a salad; the colors are nice, and the subtle heartiness of the beans creates a wonderful foundation on which the sweet muskiness of the shrimp can shine. The trick in this dish is to not overcook the beans to split pea mushiness; al dente beans have a similar texture to just-poached shrimp. Add more liquid (water is fine) toward the end of cooking the soup to prevent it from getting too thick because dried beans of different ages absorb different quantities of liquid.

MAKES 8 SERVINGS

FOR THE BEANS

1 pound dried cannellini beans
1½ tablespoons canola oil
1½ teaspoons chopped garlic
2 quarts chicken stock
1-inch rosemary sprig
1 tablespoon kosher salt

FOR THE SOUP

3 tablespoons canola oil
3 cups diced yellow onions
2 tablespoons chopped garlic
1 bay leaf
3 tablespoons chopped rosemary
2 quarts chicken stock
½ teaspoon kosher salt
¼ teaspoon white pepper
1 pound medium shrimp (31/40), peeled

To make the beans, soak them in water overnight. Heat the canola oil in a large pot over medium heat. Add the garlic and cook until soft, 2–3 minutes. Drain the beans and discard the soaking water. Add the beans, chicken stock, rosemary sprig, and salt. Bring to a simmer and cook for 40–45 minutes until the beans are al dente. If the beans are too dry, add water to keep them moist. Remove from the heat and discard the rosemary sprig.

To make the soup, in another pot, heat the canola oil over medium-high heat. Add the onions and garlic and cook until the onions are translucent, 5–7 minutes. Add the cooked beans, bay leaf, rosemary, and chicken stock and season with the salt and white pepper. Cook for 30 minutes.

Stir the shrimp into the soup and simmer until they're opaque. Remove the bay leaf and serve.

Brandied Shrimp Bisque

The beauty of this dish is that it uses leftover shrimp shells. You can incorporate poached shrimp before or after you purée the soup, but this recipe reveals just how much flavor is left in the shells. Perhaps this may be the best argument for cooking shrimp in their shells, but if you do, you won't have any shells to make this recipe. Each time I peel raw shrimp at home, I freeze the shells in a resealable freezer bag, and when I get enough, I'll make this bisque or shrimp butter (page 104). This soup also works wonderfully as a sauce for grilled or broiled fish.

MAKES 8 SERVINGS

FOR THE SHRIMP STOCK
2 tablespoons unsalted butter
2 cups shrimp shells (from approximately 5 pounds shrimp)
1 cup dry white wine
1 cup chopped leeks, green part, rinsed well
$\frac{1}{2}$ cup chopped carrots
$\frac{1}{2}$ cup chopped celery
6 cups water

FOR THE SOUP
6 tablespoons unsalted butter
$\frac{1}{2}$ cup small-diced leeks, white part, rinsed well
$\frac{1}{4}$ cup small-diced carrots
$\frac{1}{4}$ cup small-diced celery
$\frac{1}{2}$ tablespoon minced garlic
2 tablespoons tomato paste
$\frac{1}{3}$ cup rice flour

½ teaspoon tarragon
1 cup heavy cream
1 tablespoon lemon juice
Pinch of cayenne pepper
½ teaspoon smoked paprika
⅓ cup brandy

To make the shrimp stock, melt the butter in a saucepan over high heat. Add the shrimp shells, sauté until completely orange, then add the wine. Simmer until reduced by $\frac{9}{10}$, then add the leeks, carrots, and celery. Cover with the water and simmer for 45 minutes. Strain the liquid and reserve; discard the solids.

To make the soup, melt the butter in a heavy-bottomed pot over medium-low heat; sweat the leeks, carrots, and celery until soft. Add the garlic and tomato paste and cook until fragrant. Stir in the rice flour and cook for 2–3 minutes. Add the shrimp stock and tarragon; simmer for 15–20 minutes, partially covered. Add the remaining ingredients and return to a simmer.

At this point, decide if you're happy with the consistency of the soup and the showcasing of your knife work on those veggies. If you aren't happy with your handiwork, purée the soup with an immersion blender and strain out the solids. Be sure to press firmly on the solids in the strainer to extract every last bit of liquid.

Sweet Potato Soup with Ginger Shrimp

Sweet potatoes are an underappreciated pairing with the inherent sweetness and subtle texture of shrimp. Not only are they North Carolina's number one crop, but they're so versatile that April Mc-Greger wrote a Savor the South cookbook about them. Another good friend, Elizabeth Wiegand, my go-to source for all matters related to the Outer Banks of North Carolina, sent me this recipe, and I'm honored to include it here. She says, "I try to use local products as much as possible, as in local brown or green-tail shrimp from North Carolina's coast, Mattamuskeet sweet onions, and eastern North Carolina sweet potatoes. Covington or Beauregard varieties of sweet potato make a soup with a brilliant color."

MAKES 6 SERVINGS AS AN APPETIZER
OR 4 FOR LUNCH

FOR THE SOUP
1 tablespoon olive oil
1 medium sweet onion, chopped
1 teaspoon minced garlic
1 tablespoon minced ginger
About 2 pounds sweet potatoes, peeled and
   chopped into cubes
About 4 cups vegetable or chicken stock
1 teaspoon salt (or to taste)
1 teaspoon freshly ground black pepper (or to taste)

1–2 tablespoons olive oil
½ pound medium shrimp (41/50), peeled, deveined,
**   rinsed, and patted dry**
1 teaspoon minced ginger (or more if you like)
½ teaspoon minced garlic
2 teaspoons chopped chives or 2–3 green onions,
**   finely chopped**
1 tablespoon lemon juice

To make the soup, in a large pot, heat the olive oil over medium-low heat. Add the onion and stir occasionally until soft and translucent, about 5 minutes. Add the garlic and ginger and stir to coat. Add the sweet potatoes, stir, and pour in just enough vegetable or chicken stock to cover the veggies. Add the salt and pepper and stir. Bring to a simmer and cook over low heat until the sweet potatoes are fork-tender, about 30 minutes. Add more stock, if necessary, to keep the veggies covered as they cook. Purée the soup with an immersion blender until no chunks remain. Keep warm.

To make the shrimp, in a small sauté pan, heat the olive oil over medium heat. Add the shrimp and stir for 2–3 minutes until the shrimp are pink and cooked through. Add the ginger, garlic, and chives, stirring to combine. Remove from the heat and sprinkle with the lemon juice.

To serve, ladle the soup into serving bowls, then divide the shrimp evenly and place them in the center of each serving.

With Your Hands

I'm a sandwich guy. When given the opportunity, I'll
always figure out a way to combine a protein with a
starch to make a meal. Eating with your hands is casual
and fun, and I'll take messy over fussy any day. The key
to success for any sandwich is balance in every bite, so
make sure that you evenly distribute the ingredients
from end to end, whether making tacos, rolls, burgers,
or po'boys. No one wants a bite without a shrimp in
it. Two salads that could just have easily ended up in
this chapter are the Grilled Shrimp Caesar Salad (you
can put those shrimp on some toasted bread and top
them with the dressing) and the Roasted Shrimp Salad
(which is fantastic on a croissant). This chapter includes
recipes contributed by David Guas and Vivian Howard,
telegenic folks who like to eat with their hands too.

Classic Fried Shrimp Po'boys

Po'boys may be the most common way to eat shrimp in New Orleans and its environs. The original po'boy may have contained fried potatoes with roast beef gravy, but I would argue that these have become the most popular po'boys. It isn't coincidental that tomato and shrimp seasons overlap. Backyard tomatoes put these sandwiches over the top.

MAKES 4 SERVINGS

FOR THE BREADING

1 cup cornmeal

1 cup corn flour

1 tablespoon Creole seasoning (page 26)

FOR THE SANDWICHES

4 (8-inch) pieces of French bread (or French rolls
    if you don't have access to French bread)

1 pound medium shrimp (41/50), peeled

1 cup hot sauce (like Crystal), plus more to taste

2 cups breading

4 teaspoons Creole seasoning (page 26)

$\frac{1}{4}$ cup mayonnaise (not salad dressing)

Iceberg lettuce chiffonade

Vine-ripened tomatoes, sliced

To make the breading, mix all ingredients well in a shallow pan.

To make the sandwiches, heat oil in a deep fryer to 350°. Slice each piece of bread in half lengthwise. Combine the shrimp and hot sauce in a fold-top sandwich bag and shake until the shrimp are well coated. Toss the shrimp in the breading, shake off the excess, and deep-fry for 3 minutes. The sound of water bubbling up from the frying oil should diminish considerably by this point and the shrimp should float. Transfer to absorbent paper towels and sprinkle the shrimp with the Creole seasoning.

Toast the French bread and spread the mayonnaise on both cut sides. Place sliced tomatoes on the bottom pieces of bread, then place the shrimp on top of the tomatoes. Decide if you'd like to add more hot sauce, then top with the lettuce and top pieces of bread. Enjoy with cold beers.

Fire-Roasted Shrimp Tacos

These tacos are excellent for an early Sunday dinner with black beans, yellow rice, and margaritas. In this recipe, a mesh screen available at most kitchenware stores that's placed on your grill grate (whether over a wood, charcoal, or propane fire) would come in handy to keep the shrimp from falling through said grill grate. Feel free to finish your tacos anyway you prefer, but my favorite toppings are halfway between Mexican and Tex-Mex. The shrimp are also wonderful incorporated into a shrimp salad or over a Caesar salad.

MAKES 6 SERVINGS

FOR THE SHRIMP

1 tablespoon canola oil

$\frac{1}{2}$ teaspoon smoked paprika

$\frac{1}{2}$ teaspoon granulated garlic

$\frac{1}{2}$ teaspoon cumin

$\frac{1}{4}$ teaspoon ground oregano

Pinch of cayenne pepper

$\frac{1}{4}$ teaspoon freshly ground black pepper

1 teaspoon kosher salt

1 pound large shrimp (26/30), peeled

FOR THE TACOS

2 dozen corn tortillas

$\frac{1}{4}$ cup sour cream

2 avocados, pitted and sliced

4 radishes, sliced thinly, in water

1 bunch cilantro, washed and dried

2 limes, cut into 12 wedges

$\frac{1}{2}$ cup puréed salsa

To make the shrimp, fire up the grill and lower the gas flame to medium or spread coals to achieve a medium heat. Add the oil to a bowl, then stir in the seasonings. Add the shrimp and toss until well coated. Remove the shrimp from the bowl with a slotted spoon so the excess oil isn't transferred with it. Place a mesh screen on the grill, and when it's hot, put the shrimp on the screen. Cook the shrimp, turning with tongs, until orange and opaque. Transfer to a clean plate and cover with foil.

To make the tacos, divide the tortillas into 6 stacks of 4 each. Wrap each stack in aluminum foil. While the shrimp are cooking, place the 6 packets of tortillas on the grill, turning occasionally, to be warmed through.

Place the toppings in serving bowls and serve family-style with the shrimp. Give each diner a packet of tortillas. To build a taco, I recommend stacking two tortillas, smearing sour cream down the center of the top tortilla with the back of a spoon, and topping with avocado slices, then shrimp, then radishes and cilantro. Squeeze a lime wedge and/or spoon salsa on the taco just before eating.

Gulf Shrimp Rolls

I met David Guas at a party in a shepherd's field, where he arrived after a five-hour ride on a Harley to bake biscuits on a propane grill. We became fast friends. He honors both his Cuban heritage and his New Orleans roots at his rustic corner gathering place, Bayou Bakery, Coffee Bar & Eatery, in Arlington, Virginia. Guas's critically acclaimed cookbook, DamGoodSweet: Desserts to Satisfy Your Sweet Tooth, New Orleans Style, *was named one of* Food & Wine's Best New Dessert Cookbooks *of the year and was a James Beard Award finalist for best baking and dessert cookbook. This East Coast/Gulf Coast homage to the New England lobster roll will have you planning your own road trip to visit him.*

MAKES 4 SERVINGS

FOR THE SHRIMP

1 quart water

2 tablespoons paprika

1 tablespoon cayenne pepper

1 bay leaf

1 lemon, cut in half and squeezed into the liquid

¼ cup kosher salt

1 pound large shrimp (21/25), peeled

FOR THE SANDWICHES

⅓ cup mayonnaise

2 teaspoons Creole mustard

½ teaspoon celery seeds

⅛ teaspoon freshly ground black pepper

2 tablespoons thinly sliced green onions

1 tablespoon small-diced red onions

½ teaspoon hot sauce (preferably Crystal)

3 tablespoons melted unsalted butter

4 long potato rolls or hot dog buns (preferably Martin's)

To make the shrimp, combine all ingredients except the shrimp in a pot and bring to a boil. Place the shrimp in a metal or glass bowl, add the boiling liquid, stir, and cover for 5–7 minutes. Drain the shrimp and chill for 30–45 minutes in the refrigerator.

To assemble the sandwiches, chop the shrimp. Mix all remaining ingredients except the melted butter and rolls in a bowl. Using a rubber spatula, stir in the shrimp and mix well. Brush the melted butter on the inside of each roll and broil in the oven just until crisp and slightly browned, 2–3 minutes. Be careful not to place the rack too close to the broiler and check on the rolls throughout the toasting process. Remove the rolls from the oven and place approximately ½ cup of the shrimp mixture on each roll.

Shrimp Burgers with Boiler Room Tartar Sauce, Tomatoes, and Arugula

This recipe comes from Vivian Howard, the chef/owner of Chef & the Farmer in Kinston, North Carolina. She recounts, "Every time I go to the beach here, I have to have a shrimp burger. Nostalgia brings me back year after year, but I hate how the little shrimp are always slipping out of the sides of my burger and ending up in my lap. So the idea for the shrimp patty was born." Her shrimp patties are dredged in cracker meal for that authentic touch.

MAKES 6 SERVINGS

FOR THE TARTAR SAUCE

1 cup mayonnaise (preferably Duke's)
½ cup sour cream
⅓ cup lemon juice
½ cup pickle relish (Vivian uses a sweetish tarragon pickle relish)
1 tablespoon rice vinegar
1 tablespoon chopped parsley
2 tablespoons chopped tarragon
1 tablespoon chopped mint
Few dashes of Tabasco sauce
2 tablespoons chopped capers
1 tablespoon caper brine
1 teaspoon kosher salt

FOR THE SHRIMP BURGERS

3 tablespoons vegetable oil, divided
1 medium onion, minced
1 large celery stalk, minced
1 medium carrot, minced
4 garlic cloves, minced
1 pound medium shrimp (31/40), peeled and deveined

1 large egg, beaten
3 tablespoons cracker meal, plus more for dredging
Zest of 1 lemon
2 tablespoons roasted garlic purée
1 tablespoon sriracha sauce
2 teaspoons kosher salt
6 hamburger buns
Sliced tomatoes seasoned with salt, pepper, and sugar
Arugula dressed with lemon juice and salt

To make the tartar sauce, whisk all the ingredients together in a bowl and let chill for at least 1 hour before using.

To make the shrimp burgers, in a medium sauté pan, heat 1 tablespoon of the oil slightly and add the onion, celery, and carrot. Sweat over medium-low heat for about 10 minutes, or until they begin to soften. Add the minced garlic and continue to cook for 2 minutes. Spread this mixture on a baking sheet and allow it to cool to room temperature.

When cool, place the mixture in a food processor and add ⅔ of the shrimp. Blend until smooth; you shouldn't have any large chunks of shrimp or vegetables. Cut the remaining ⅓ of the shrimp into ¼-inch pieces. Transfer the mixture to a large bowl and stir in the cut-up shrimp, egg, cracker meal, lemon zest, garlic purée, sriracha, and salt. Allow the mixture to rest for about 20 minutes, then form 6 patties using a ½-cup scoop and dredge them in cracker meal.

To cook the burgers, heat the remaining 2 tablespoons of oil in a large sauté pan until shimmering. Add the patties and cook 3–4 minutes on each side. Serve each patty on a steamed bun with a generous helping of tartar sauce, sliced tomatoes, and arugula.

With Noodles

This book easily could have contained fifty shrimp pasta recipes if I had chosen to include all of the permutations of shrimp plus sauce plus noodles. So I thought I would focus on a few special recipes. The carbonara is great in spring because that's when North Carolina calico scallops become available. The angel hair dish is best in late summer when you're looking for new ways to eat cherry tomatoes. My dad's dish is good just about anytime, but it really hits the spot in the fall.

Garlicky Shrimp with Angel Hair Pasta

This dish is a bit of a contrast to the hearty, bold flavors that get paired with shrimp in some recipes in this book. The Confit Cherry Tomatoes are a nod to California cuisine, and their sweetness enhances that of the shrimp. The oil from the confit gives body to the pan sauce, and the lemon juice brightens the whole dish. This is a wonderful summertime entrée eaten al fresco accompanied by a Caesar salad.

MAKES 4 SERVINGS

FOR THE CONFIT CHERRY TOMATOES
(MAKES 2 CUPS)

1 pint cherry tomatoes
5 tablespoons light brown sugar
1 cup olive oil
2 teaspoons minced garlic
1 teaspoon small-diced red onions
3 basil leaves
½ teaspoon kosher salt

FOR THE PASTA

2 tablespoons canola oil
2 tablespoons minced garlic
1 pound small shrimp (71/90), peeled
1 tablespoon kosher salt
1 teaspoon freshly ground black pepper
¾ cup chicken broth
2 tablespoons lemon juice
1 cup Confit Cherry Tomatoes plus ¼ cup of their oil
½ pound angel hair pasta, cooked according to
    package directions
2 tablespoons grated Parmesan
2 tablespoons chopped green onions

To make the Confit Cherry Tomatoes, place all ingredients in a saucepan on a burner on the lowest possible setting; setting the pan over a pilot light is ideal. Allow to sit undisturbed until the oil begins to bubble, which means the tomatoes have reached about 212°. Remove from the heat and cool to room temperature. Remove the basil leaves and discard. Store in the refrigerator in a container that prevents the tomatoes from breaking the surface of the oil.

To make the pasta, heat the oil in a sauté pan over medium heat. Add the garlic and cook until fragrant and golden, 2–3 minutes. Season the shrimp with the salt and pepper, then add to the sauté pan. Toss to coat the shrimp in the garlic. Cook until the shrimp are seared but not fully cooked. Deglaze the pan with the chicken broth and lemon juice, scraping the bottom to loosen any stuck bits. Simmer until the liquid is reduced by half. Add the tomatoes and their oil; heat through.

Divide the cooked pasta between 4 serving bowls, twisting and mounding it in the center. Place the shrimp-tomato mixture over the pasta And sprinkle with the Parmesan and green onions.

NOTE ❋ Leftover Confit Cherry Tomatoes are great mixed with mozzarella cubes for bruschetta.

Calabash Cajun Carbonara

Carbonara allegedly was invented for American GIs in Italy during World War II utilizing ingredients they knew from home—ham and eggs. Perhaps this is more romantic myth than fact, but who can argue with the results? Regardless of carbonara's origins, cooking the eggs gently with the heat from the hot pasta results in a warm, velvet-textured sauce that reminds us that not everything we eat should be piping hot or ice cold—happiness is often found in the middle. Calabash is on the North Carolina coast and is synonymous with heaping mixed-seafood platters, and the Cajun tasso ham contributes a refreshing complexity.

MAKES 4 SERVINGS

2 tablespoons canola oil

3 ounces tasso ham, julienned

3/4 pound large shrimp (21/25), peeled

3/4 pound calico scallops (or bay scallops)

2 teaspoons kosher salt

1/4 cup chopped green onions

1/4 cup chicken broth

1 tablespoon lemon juice

1 pound fettuccine, cooked according to package directions

2 large eggs

1/4 cup heavy cream

1 tablespoon grated Parmesan

Heat the oil in a heavy-bottomed pot over medium-high heat; add the tasso ham and sauté. Add the shrimp and scallops and sprinkle with the salt. Cook until the seafood is about 75 percent done, then add the green onions, chicken broth, lemon juice, and pasta. Cook until the broth is mostly evaporated; remove from the heat.

Meanwhile, beat the eggs and cream in a large heatproof bowl. Remove the hot pasta from the pot with tongs, place it in the egg mixture, and toss well. The heat from the pasta will cook the eggs. Transfer the pasta to 4 serving bowls and distribute the seafood mixture over it. Garnish with the Parmesan.

Shrimp Linguine

This recipe is my father, William Pierce's, current version of a dish we enjoyed in my youth that we used to call shrimp Alfredo. I don't remember it containing nearly as much green stuff, but times have changed. The flavor is much richer if you have the opportunity to use head-on shrimp, but it takes a deft touch to eat head-on shrimp when tossed with linguine. We aren't ashamed to use our hands and suck our fingers. This dish is also good with egg noodles and with smaller shrimp, making it a side dish instead of an entrée.

MAKES 4 SERVINGS

3 pounds jumbo shrimp (16/20), peeled, head-on, or
    1½ pounds large shrimp (26/30), peeled, deheaded
1 tablespoon Creole seasoning (page 26)
1 teaspoon kosher salt
1 stick unsalted butter
3 tablespoons olive oil
1 cup chopped green onions, divided
1 tablespoon chopped garlic
1 tablespoon chopped parsley, divided
1 cup heavy whipping cream
2 pinches cayenne pepper
½ pound linguine, cooked according to package directions

Season the shrimp with the Creole seasoning and salt. In a heavy skillet, melt the butter with the olive oil over high heat. Add ¾ cup of the green onions, the garlic, and half of the parsley; sauté for 1 minute. Add the cream, keeping the skillet on high heat. Add the shrimp and stir until they're pink all over and the mixture is reduced, about 3 minutes. Add the cayenne pepper and the remaining green onions and parsley. Cook for 1 minute.

Remove the skillet from the heat and add the pasta, tossing to coat it with the sauce. Divide the pasta between 4 plates and top with the shrimp and sauce.

With Rice

When I was growing up in South Louisiana, we had rice just about every night, always long-grain white rice. I've since learned to enjoy many different varieties of rice, but if the type of rice isn't specified in the following recipes, I suggest using jasmine rice. I've included a pilaf-style recipe for making plain white rice (page 92), but it's also acceptable to cook this starchy staple in a rice steamer or a microwave. Do what you know.

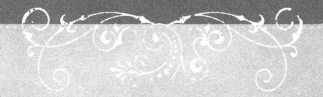

Jambalaya

I grew up eating jambalaya without realizing how special it was. Since then, I've witnessed the adulteration of jambalaya, simply a pilaf with Cajun seasonings and flavorful meat, in many places outside the home. Paul Prudhomme has said that the only things he puts tomatoes in are salads, and the addition of tomato is where most folks go astray with jambalaya. The color of the dish is achieved by sautéing the rice in the paprika-infused oil, and the sweetness comes from the green bell peppers and shrimp. Adding tomato to this dish is a superficial shortcut. Here's a tip: if you make your own chicken stock, replace the canola oil in this recipe with the congealed fat from the top of your refrigerated stock. Building flavor is the name of the game.

MAKES 6 SERVINGS

5 tablespoons canola oil, divided
10 ounces andouille sausage, cut in half and sliced
    ¼ inch thick
1 pound boneless chicken, chopped
⅓ cup chopped green bell peppers
½ cup chopped yellow onions
⅓ cup chopped celery
1 teaspoon minced garlic
2 cups long-grain white rice
1 teaspoon paprika
1 tablespoon Creole seasoning (page 26)
1 bay leaf
1 pound medium shrimp (31/40), peeled
4 cups chicken broth
Kosher salt and freshly ground black pepper

Heat 2 tablespoons of the oil in a large skillet over medium-high heat. Add the sausage and chicken and sauté until browned on all sides. Remove the meats to a plate. In the same skillet, add the remaining 3 tablespoons oil. Add the green bell peppers, onions, and celery. Sauté for 5 minutes, or until tender. Add the garlic, rice, and spices and continue stirring until the oil has coated all of the rice and the garlic is fragrant, about 3 minutes. Return the chicken and sausage to the skillet and add the shrimp. Add the chicken broth, turn the heat down to low, and cover. Simmer until all of the liquid is absorbed, 10–15 minutes. Remove the bay leaf and add salt and pepper to taste. Add additional chicken broth if needed. Allow the finished dish to rest off the heat for about 5 minutes, then fluff with a fork before serving.

NOTE ❋ If you don't trust your stove to maintain an even heat or if you're scaling up this recipe to feed a crowd, after you add the broth, the dish can be baked at 350° in a covered, oven-proof dish for about the same time. The bottom is less likely to burn, and the steady heat will ensure that all of the liquid is absorbed.

Shrimp Country Captain

Country captain is a classic preparation from Charleston, South Carolina, that usually features chicken. This recipe brings together that tradition with a Jamaican curried shrimp that I learned while working in Eugene, Oregon. This is truly a melting-pot dish.

MAKES 4 SERVINGS

2 tablespoons canola oil

2½ teaspoons curry powder

½ cup diced yellow onions

½ cup diced carrots

½ cup diced green bell peppers

1 pound jumbo shrimp (16/20), peeled, head-on, with tails left on

2 teaspoons kosher salt

2 teaspoons freshly ground black pepper

1 teaspoon grated ginger

1 tablespoon minced garlic

¾ cup chopped tomatoes

3½ cups vegetable stock

½ cup coconut milk

1½ tablespoons dry sherry

¼ teaspoon Tabasco sauce

Cooked rice

¼ cup raisins

¼ cup chopped green onions

¼ cup toasted sliced almonds

Heat the oil in a skillet over medium heat. Whisk in the curry powder and cook for 4 minutes, or until darkened and fragrant. Add the onions, carrots, and bell peppers and sauté for about 10 minutes until wilted. Season the shrimp with salt and pepper and add to the skillet, browning on each side. Add the ginger, garlic, and tomatoes and cook for another 5 minutes. Add the vegetable stock and bring to a simmer. Stir in the coconut milk and sherry. Simmer until thickened. Stir in the Tabasco sauce.

Mound rice on a family-style platter and top with the shrimp mixture. Garnish with raisins, green onions, and almonds.

Creamed Rice with Spicy Sausage and Shrimp

This recipe comes from a good friend, Jason Alley, who is the chef/ partner of Comfort and Pasture restaurants in Richmond, Virginia. We met on a Southern Foodways Alliance field trip to Bristol, Virginia, and hit it off instantly. At each of his restaurants, Jason updates southern classics using locally sourced ingredients and impeccable technique. This dish has all the makings of a Low Country purloo but hews to no tradition.

MAKES 4 SERVINGS

3 cups chicken stock

1 cup tomato juice

1 tablespoon vegetable oil

1½ cups basmati rice

½ pound hot Italian sausage, removed from the casing

½ pound large shrimp (21/25), peeled

½ cup heavy cream

2 tablespoons unsalted butter

2 teaspoons kosher salt

1 teaspoon freshly ground black pepper

¼ cup grated Romano, divided

¼ cup sliced green onions, divided

Combine the chicken stock and tomato juice in a large saucepan and warm. Place a heavy-bottomed pot over medium-high heat, add the oil, and heat through. Sauté the rice until translucent; using a large ladle, add enough of the stock/tomato juice mixture to just cover the rice. Reduce the heat to a simmer and gradually add all but ½ cup of the stock/tomato mixture, stirring constantly. When the rice is just cooked, transfer it to a bowl.

Heat another pan large enough to hold the rice over medium-high heat. Add the sausage and cook until just browned. Add the shrimp and cook until they just turn translucent. Add the reserved stock/tomato juice mixture and cream. Add the rice and butter and stir until heated through. Season with the salt and pepper.

Divide between 4 hot bowls and garnish with the Romano and green onions.

Buttered Brown Rice with Shrimp, Duck Cracklings, and Roasted Mushrooms

I'm often amazed at the wonderful people I meet where food and books intersect. I met Gabrielle Hamilton, chef/owner of Prune restaurant in New York City, while she was on tour with her first book, and we've continued to stay in touch. She graciously contributed the following recipe for this book. The layers of flavor in this dish and the rustic simplicity of its presentation speak volumes about her approach to food and its place in our lives.

MAKES 4 SERVINGS

Skins from 2 large duck breasts
1 tablespoon plus 1½ teaspoons kosher salt, divided
5 cups plus ⅓ cup water, divided
3 star anise pods, divided
1 cup brown rice
6 tablespoons unsalted butter, divided
½ pound honshimiji mushrooms (or other wild mushrooms)
2 tablespoons olive oil
¼ teaspoon freshly ground black pepper
1 pound small shrimp (71/90), peeled and deveined
4 scallions, green part, wide bias-cut (same size as the shrimp)

In a skillet over medium-low heat, render the duck skins slowly until crispy and thoroughly golden with almost no subcutaneous fat left. Drain off the fat as it accumulates so the skins don't fry in their own fat. Remove from the skillet and drain on paper towels. Season with ½ teaspoon of the salt while warm and, when cool enough to handle, cut into strips.

Bring 5 cups of the water to a rolling boil. Season with 1 tablespoon of the salt and 1 star anise pod. Add the brown rice and boil uncovered until tender and chewy, approximately 25 minutes. Drain in a colander, then return to the pot and add 2 tablespoons of the butter, stirring gently to coat each grain. Keep warm.

Trim the mushrooms and separate the clump into manageable segments. (If you use shiitakes, remove the stems and slice the caps into ⅓-inch strips.) Toss the mushrooms with the olive oil, season with 1 teaspoon of the salt and the pepper, and roast in a 450° oven until they take on color, are fully cooked, and start to crisp up.

Boil the remaining ⅓ cup of water in a very small saucepan with 1 star anise pod. Allow to boil until reduced to less than ¼ cup and until you detect a strong aroma of star anise. Turn off the heat and add 2 tablespoons of the butter, whisking constantly until the butter is fully melted and you have a loose but creamy and glossy beurre fondue. Season with a pinch of salt.

Melt the remaining 2 tablespoons of butter in a large, wide sauté pan over medium-high heat with the remaining star anise pod. Add the shrimp and scallions and sauté for about 2 minutes until the shrimp are cooked but still vital and juicy and the scallions are soft but still green and vibrant. Add the roasted mushrooms and toss them with the shrimp and scallions.

Spoon the warm brown rice into 4 wide bowls, divide the shrimp and mushroom mixture evenly between the bowls, and spoon the star anise beurre fondue over the 4 portions. Finish each bowl with duck cracklings.

Lemony Shrimp Risotto

Three things to note about this recipe: citrus and seafood work wonderfully together, a key to success is warm broth and coating the rice in butter, and apparently I have a blatant disregard for the Italian adage that fish and cheese should never be combined in the same dish. Perhaps shrimp are an exception. Preserved lemons are a wonderful item to have in your fridge; they can be used in seafood dishes to lend an exotic, fragrant saltiness. If you can't find any, make your own; you won't regret it.

MAKES 4 SERVINGS

6 cups shrimp broth

1 stick unsalted butter

2 tablespoons minced garlic

1 tablespoon rinsed, minced preserved lemons

2 cups Arborio rice

¼ cup dry vermouth

1 pound medium shrimp (31/40), peeled

½ teaspoon white pepper

1 cup grated Pecorino Romano

2 teaspoons kosher salt

2 tablespoons basil chiffonade

2 tablespoons lemon juice

4 teaspoons grated lemon peel (a microplane works best)

Heat the shrimp broth in a saucepan and keep warm. Melt the butter in a heavy-bottomed pan (a sautoir is best for this) over medium heat. Add the garlic and preserved lemons; sauté until fragrant and golden, about 5 minutes. Add the rice, stirring to ensure that every grain is coated in butter. Add the vermouth and cook until evaporated, about 30 seconds. Add 2 cups of the warm broth; simmer until absorbed, stirring frequently. Add the remaining broth 1 cup at a time, allowing the broth to be absorbed completely before adding more. When half of the broth has been added and the pan is dry, add the shrimp and white pepper with the next addition of broth. Continue stirring and adding broth until all of the broth has been added. Stir in the cheese and salt. Stir in the basil, lemon juice, and lemon peel.

Shrimp and Okra

In this dish, I take two things I know and love and encourage them to get together. There's always frozen, cut okra in my freezer (you never know when the urge to cook gumbo will strike), so I've gotten in the habit of adding a small amount of leftover okra to a quick shrimp Creole preparation for texture and because who doesn't love okra smothered in tomato sauce? The resulting dish was a revelation—quick and easy and oh so tasty.

MAKES 4 SERVINGS

FOR THE RICE

1 tablespoon canola oil
1 cup long-grain rice
1 teaspoon kosher salt
2 cups water

FOR THE SHRIMP

1 pound large shrimp (21/25), peeled
1½ tablespoons Creole seasoning (page 26)
¼ cup plus 1 tablespoon canola oil, divided
½ cup medium-diced celery
½ cup medium-diced green bell peppers
1 cup medium-diced yellow onions
½ pound okra, sliced (thawed if frozen)
2 teaspoons minced garlic
2 cups crushed tomatoes
1 cup chopped tomatoes in purée
1 cup V8 juice
2 tablespoons chopped green onions

To make the rice, in a heavy-bottomed saucepan, heat the oil over medium heat. Add the rice and salt and stir until well coated. Add the water and bring to a boil, then lower the heat, cover, and simmer for 10 minutes, or until all of the water is absorbed. How can you tell if the liquid is absorbed if you don't peek? Hold the lid down and shake the pot gently. If it sloshes, the rice isn't done yet. If it feels solid, remove from the heat and let rest 5 minutes without removing the lid, then fluff with a fork.

Meanwhile, to make the shrimp, season it with the Creole seasoning. Heat ¼ cup of the oil in a Dutch oven over medium heat. Add the celery, green bell peppers, and onions and cook until soft. Add the okra and garlic and cook 5–7 minutes until the garlic is fragrant. Add both types of tomatoes and the V8 juice and bring to a simmer.

Heat the remaining 1 tablespoon canola oil in a nonstick sauté pan over high heat. Add the shrimp and sauté until the spices are toasted and the shrimp are opaque. Add the shrimp to the simmering sauce and cook 5 more minutes.

Place the rice in 4 bowls. Ladle the shrimp mixture over the rice. Garnish with the green onions.

Esma's Shrimp Stew

My mother's grandmother was the benchmark cook in our family; everyone still compares their cooking to hers. Esma Richoux was born in LaRose, Louisiana, where she was head of the household by the age of sixteen. After relocating to the suburbs of New Orleans with her husband, Norba Trosclair, she hosted all of our family's memorable meals. She was allergic to shrimp, so this is based on her chicken stew recipe. My mother, Collette Boudreaux, loves shrimp, so she omitted the lima beans and chicken and added shrimp. My mother's rendition of this dish is what ignited the passion for food that burns in me today.

MAKES 8 SERVINGS

3/4 cup canola oil

3/4 cup all-purpose flour

1 medium onion, chopped

3/4 cup chopped celery

2 garlic cloves, minced

1 small green bell pepper, chopped

2 cups chicken broth

1 cup water

2 teaspoons kosher salt

Freshly ground black pepper

1 teaspoon thyme

4 bay leaves

1 tablespoon Creole seasoning (page 26)

2 pounds large shrimp (26/30), peeled

2 tablespoons chopped parsley

Combine the oil and flour in a cast-iron skillet over medium heat. Stir, slowly and constantly, until the roux is the color of chocolate, 20–30 minutes. Add the onion, celery, garlic, and bell pepper, mix well, and remove from the heat.

When the vegetables stop sizzling and producing steam, transfer the mixture to a Dutch oven or similar-sized heavy-bottomed pot. Gradually add the chicken stock (you may add water as needed—the stew should be thinner now than you want the end result to be).

Add the salt, pepper, thyme, bay leaves, and Creole seasoning. Bring to a boil, then reduce the heat to medium-low. Add the shrimp and simmer for 15–20 minutes. Remove the bay leaves and add the parsley in the last few minutes. Serve over rice.

Shrimp Étouffée

Beth Newcombe Abadie is a cook's cook. She loves to eat, but she loves to cook for other people even more. Born and raised in the heart of New Orleans, she began cooking at a young age. Barely tall enough to see the burners, she decided that if she wanted to eat better food, she needed to learn to make it herself. Her étouffée recipe has a nice kick to it, from both the jalapeño and the brandy.

MAKES 4–6 SERVINGS

1 stick unsalted butter
4 tablespoons flour
1 tablespoon cornstarch
1 large onion, chopped
1 red bell pepper, chopped
1 jalapeño pepper, chopped
1 shallot, chopped
2 stalks celery, chopped
3 garlic cloves, chopped
1 tablespoon chopped parsley
1 tablespoon chopped basil
1 teaspoon chopped thyme
1 teaspoon kosher salt
$\frac{1}{2}$ teaspoon cayenne pepper (or to taste)
1 teaspoon freshly ground black pepper
4 cups chicken or shrimp stock
1 teaspoon Lea & Perrins Worcestershire sauce
3 pounds medium shrimp (41/50), peeled
$\frac{1}{2}$ cup brandy

In a 4–5-quart, preferably cast-iron pot, melt the butter. Add the flour and cornstarch and cook over low heat, stirring constantly until the mixture is a deep, rich brown color. Add the onion, red bell pepper, jalapeño, shallot, celery, and garlic. Sauté until tender. Add the parsley, basil, thyme, salt, and both peppers and cook until aromatic, stirring frequently, about 3–5 minutes. Add the chicken or shrimp stock and Worcestershire sauce and bring to a boil. Reduce the heat and let simmer for 20 minutes, stirring often. Add the shrimp and brandy and stir well. Cook another 20 minutes over low heat until the shrimp are done. Serve over rice.

Composed Dishes

Most of the recipes in this chapter are a bit more in-
volved than those in other chapters, but the extra effort
will be rewarded with memorable dishes. Assembling
the enchiladas may take a bit of practice, but the results
are well worth the effort. The shrimp butter is another
recipe that uses shrimp shells. You'll want to make
enough butter to keep in your freezer so you can to whip
it out as a trump card for some unsuspecting meal. The
book concludes with Shrimp and Grits, the dish that's
popping up on every southern menu.

Shrimp and Spinach Enchiladas

A favorite Sunday exercise, this recipe takes a little time to prepare, but it's soul-satisfying. Don't worry about making too many enchiladas; these are wonderful as leftovers with a little microwaving. A margarita makes an ideal pairing.

MAKES 4 SERVINGS

FOR THE CHILI SAUCE

3 dried guajillo chilies

1 dried chipotle chili

2 cups water

1 tablespoon canola oil

½ cup chopped carrots

½ medium onion, chopped

¼ cup tomato purée

2 garlic cloves, smashed

½ teaspoon kosher salt

Juice of ½ lime

FOR THE ENCHILADAS

1 (10-ounce) box frozen chopped spinach

15 ounces whole milk ricotta cheese

8 ounces sour cream

1½ teaspoons granulated garlic

½ teaspoon coriander

½ teaspoon oregano

1½ teaspoons kosher salt

¼ teaspoon freshly ground black pepper

½ teaspoon cumin

1 tablespoon Goya Recaito (a cilantro-based purée)

1 pound small shrimp (71/90), peeled

2 tablespoons Creole seasoning (page 26)

1 tablespoon canola oil

24 (6-inch) corn tortillas

1 cup grated Pepper Jack cheese

To make the chili sauce, in a small saucepan over medium heat, add both types of chilies. Toast until fragrant, then add the water and simmer until the chilies are soft, about 5 minutes. Pour the liquid and chilies into a bowl and allow to rest.

Add the oil to the saucepan and return to medium heat; add the carrots and onion and cook until soft, about 7 minutes. Add the tomato purée, garlic, and salt and cook for 3 minutes. Reserving the water, remove the stems and seeds from the chilies and chop the flesh. Add the chilies and reserved water to the saucepan. Bring to a simmer and cook for 20 minutes. Purée with an immersion blender and add the lime juice.

To make the enchiladas, in a small saucepan, add ¼ cup water and the frozen spinach, boil covered for 5 minutes, then strain in a colander. Using the back of a spoon, press as much water out of the spinach as possible.

In a bowl, whisk together the ricotta cheese, sour cream, granulated garlic, coriander, oregano, salt, pepper, cumin, and Recaito. When well combined, add the spinach; mix well.

In a separate bowl, combine the shrimp and Creole seasoning. Heat the oil in a nonstick pan over medium-high heat and sauté the shrimp until cooked through. Allow the shrimp to cool a bit before adding to the spinach mixture.

Preheat the oven to 350°. Set up a station next to your stove, in this order: a dry cast-iron skillet on a low burner, a clean plate, the shrimp-spinach mixture, a 9 × 13-inch baking dish, and an 8 × 8-inch baking dish. In the skillet, warm the tortillas on each side, one at a time, then transfer to the plate. Spoon a heaping tablespoon of the filling into the center of each tortilla, roll it up, and place it in a baking dish with the loose end down. Repeat until you've used all of the filling. I normally get between 20 and 24 enchiladas. Pour the chili sauce over the tortillas. Bake uncovered for 20 minutes. Remove from the oven, sprinkle with the cheese, and serve with beans and saffron rice.

Cajun Shrimp Boil

The fundamental difference between a Cajun shrimp boil and a Low Country shrimp boil is the amount of seasoning in the pot. The oversize pots on propane burners around both Charleston and New Orleans usually contain corn on the cob, new potatoes, pork sausage (like kielbasa), garlic bulbs, lemons, cayenne pepper, and water so salty it tastes like the sea. Folks in South Louisiana have a tendency to tip a bit more of that garnet-colored powder into just about everything they cook. Secondarily, whereas South Carolinians hew to tradition, a Cajun boil often includes unexpected additions to the pot—I've witnessed brussels sprouts, mushrooms, olives, and hot dogs, among other things. Don't worry about what it's called; do what you like and have fun. My brother Christian helped me test this recipe because he loves gatherings of like-minded folk and conversations over homebrew and spicy crustaceans as much as I do. This recipe can be scaled up to feed as many people as you want, and you can dial back the cayenne to suit your needs. I wouldn't recommend reducing the salt; it just can't be added later.

MAKES 8 SERVINGS

---

9 gallons water

¾ cup cayenne pepper

8 cups sea salt, divided

1 cup coriander seeds

¾ cup celery seeds

12 lemons, cut in half

1 cup bay leaves

1 pound garlic bulbs, top end trimmed to expose cloves

6 medium yellow onions, quartered

2 pounds smoked pork sausage links (kielbasa is great), cut into 2-inch chunks

5 pounds small new potatoes
10 pounds medium-to-large shrimp (31/40 or 26/30), unpeeled
10 ears corn, shucked, cut in half

In a large stockpot (I use a 100-quart pot; in South Louisiana, you can find these for sale in just about every outdoor goods store) on an outdoor propane ring, bring the water, cayenne pepper, 6 cups of the sea salt, coriander seeds, celery seeds, lemon halves, and bay leaves to a boil. Lower the heat to a simmer and cook for 30 minutes with the lid on.

Place the strainer basket into the stockpot and add the garlic, onions, sausage, and potatoes. Simmer with the lid on for 20 minutes; check a potato to make sure it's done. Lift the strainer basket and allow the excess liquid to run back into the pot. Scatter the contents of the strainer onto a newspaper-covered table.

Return the strainer to the pot, add the remaining 2 cups of sea salt, bring the liquid to a boil, and add all of the shrimp at once. Return the liquid to a simmer, cook for 2 minutes, turn off the flame, add the corn, cover, and allow to soak for 15 minutes. Lift the strainer basket, allowing the liquid to drain back into the pot, and spill the shrimp over the vegetables on the newspaper-lined table. Peel, eat, and enjoy.

NOTE ✻ If you have leftovers, here are some suggestions. The potatoes make great potato salad. The shrimp can be used in a few recipes in this book. The corn can be cut from the cob and combined with the onions, the garlic, and some butter to make an amazing side dish. The sausage can be split and pan-fried for a quick sandwich.

Grilled Steaks with Shrimp Butter

This is another recipe that uses shrimp shells instead of shrimp, this time to produce a flavor bomb you can keep in the freezer and whip out when you want to blow minds. The shrimp butter is fantastic when used to finish seafood pasta or risotto. The ultimate might be these ribeyes. I like to cook the steaks outside because the exhaust fans in most homes can't handle the amount of smoke generated from properly searing a steak. If you prefer to substitute a different cut of steak for the ribeyes, you may need to drizzle the steaks with a little bit of oil before cooking them.

MAKES 4 SERVINGS

FOR THE SHRIMP BUTTER

1 teaspoon canola oil
1/4 cup minced yellow onions
1/2 cup shrimp shells
1/4 cup dry white wine or dry vermouth
1 stick unsalted butter, at room temperature
1/4 teaspoon smoked paprika
1/4 teaspoon sea salt

FOR THE STEAKS

4 ribeye steaks, 1 inch thick
Kosher salt
Freshly ground black pepper

To make the shrimp butter, heat the canola oil in a heavy-bottomed pot over medium heat; add the onions and cook until soft. Add the shrimp shells and stir until the shells are bright orange. Add the wine and simmer until reduced by ⅞. Set a fine-mesh strainer over a bowl, transfer the contents of the pot to the strainer, and press with the back of a spoon to extract every drop of liquid. Discard the solids.

Place the butter in a stand mixer with the paddle attachment and mix on low. Add the paprika, salt, and shrimp reduction; mix until well combined.

Place a piece of wax paper or parchment paper on the counter. Transfer the butter to the paper and roll up into a log, twisting the ends like taffy. The diameter should be about the size of a quarter. Date the butter log and freeze until ready for use.

To make the steaks, season both sides of the steaks liberally with salt and pepper. Allow the steaks to rest at room temperature for about 30 minutes before cooking.

Fire up your propane grill and place 2 large cast-iron skillets or a cast-iron griddle on it. Heat the skillets or griddle until they're smoking. Place 2 steaks into each of the skillets or 4 steaks on the griddle. For rare steaks, sear hard on each side; for medium, the bottom third of the steaks should be cooked before flipping; for well done, the steaks should be cooked beyond the midpoint before flipping. Carefully flip the steaks, mindful of the rendered fat, and get a good sear on the second side. Remove the steaks to a clean plate and allow to rest for 5 minutes or so. Serve each steak topped with a slice of frozen shrimp butter and a baked potato or egg noodles with more of the shrimp butter.

Shrimp-Stuffed Pork Chops

The inspiration for this recipe is the crawfish bread that's often available at the annual New Orleans Jazz and Heritage Festival, which features a jaw-dropping array of culinary delights. To re-create this bread, split a length of airy French bread and fill with the shrimp stuffing, wrap in foil, and bake until aromatic. Perhaps even more fun is to mix ½ cup panko breadcrumbs with the shrimp stuffing, form into 3-ounce cakes, dredge in more breadcrumbs, bake until warm, and serve with a spicy tomato-based sauce. Once you try this method of stuffing, you may not go back to cutting pockets in chops. This is easier to prep and cook, and you get so much more stuffing in each serving.

MAKES 8 SERVINGS

FOR THE STUFFING

1 pound small shrimp (71/90), peeled
¾ teaspoon Creole seasoning (page 26)
2 tablespoons unsalted butter
¼ cup diced yellow onions
¼ cup diced celery
¼ cup diced red bell peppers
½ tablespoon minced garlic
¼ teaspoon dry mustard
¼ cup mayonnaise
¼ cup grated provolone cheese
¼ cup grated cheddar cheese
½ teaspoon Lea & Perrins Worcestershire sauce
½ teaspoon Tabasco sauce

8 pork chops, 1 inch thick
Kosher salt
Freshly ground black pepper
2 tablespoons canola oil
½ cup Italian-style breadcrumbs

To make the stuffing, season the shrimp with the Creole seasoning. In a sauté pan, melt the butter over medium heat. Add the onions, celery, and peppers and cook until soft, 4–5 minutes. Add the shrimp and sauté until opaque. The pan should be dry at this point; if there's excess liquid in the pan, continue cooking to evaporate the liquid before moving on. Stir in the garlic and mustard, remove from the heat, and place in a bowl. Allow the mixture to cool slightly. Add the mayonnaise, cheeses, Worcestershire sauce, and Tabasco sauce. Combine well and refrigerate.

To make the pork chops, preheat the oven to 350°. Season both sides of the pork chops with salt and pepper. Heat a cast-iron skillet over medium-high heat; when hot, add the oil. In batches, sear the pork chops, about 1 minute on each side. Transfer the seared pork chops to a baking pan. Top each pork chop with ½ cup shrimp stuffing. Sprinkle breadcrumbs over each mound of stuffing, allowing the excess to fall onto the bottom of the pan. Bake the pork chops until the stuffing has slumped, about 12 minutes. The pork chops should be medium well. Transfer to plates and serve.

Southwestern Shrimp Stew

My colleague and good friend Michael Ruoss crafted this recipe. It's a crowd pleaser that's as unconventional as he is. He rose to the pinnacle of his profession as the chef de cuisine of my favorite restaurant in New Orleans and then decided to shift gears to spend time with his girls as they were growing up, yet somehow he is overseeing more restaurants. This recipe is easy to make and fun to eat, dipping and slurping and carrying on.

MAKES 6–8 HEARTY SERVINGS

---

1 cup diced tomatoes
1 cup julienned red bell peppers
1 cup julienned red onions
½ cup chopped cilantro
½ cup chopped parsley
4 tablespoons minced chipotle peppers in adobo
2 tablespoons kosher salt
1 cup extra-virgin olive oil
1 tablespoon cumin
2 cups sliced andouille sausage (or kielbasa)
2 cups chicken broth
2 cups dry white wine
2 cups seafood broth (shrimp stock would be great)
2 pounds jumbo shrimp (U15), peeled and deveined

In a bowl, mix the tomatoes, red bell peppers, red onions, cilantro, parsley, chipotle peppers, salt, olive oil, cumin, and sausage. Refrigerate for at least 2 hours.

In a large saucepan, bring to a boil the chicken broth, wine, and seafood broth. Add the sausage mixture and simmer for 10 minutes. Add the shrimp and simmer for 5 minutes, or until the shrimp are fully cooked. Serve in bowls with toasted French bread.

Shrimp and Grits

How did a humble fisherman's breakfast become the ubiquitous southern offering on menus across the United States? What began as shrimp cooked in bacon drippings and served over grits by men who caught said crustaceans from Charleston to St. Augustine has evolved into a $30 entrée with heirloom grains and truffled emulsions. Shrimp and grits' status has risen so much recently that the dish garnered more votes than pulled pork barbecue in Garden & Gun *magazine's 2011 Southern Foods Championship, in which readers weighed in on what they believed to be the most iconic dish in the South.*

The essential components of traditional shrimp and grits are onions, plump shrimp, fatty smoked pork, toothsome grits, and silky gravy. Common additions include mushrooms, roasted peppers, and cream. As with most dishes of humble origin, fewer ingredients of higher quality usually result in a superior preparation. At its foundation, the unbilled pork elevates the gravy with its smoky unctuousness, the delicate flavors of the shrimp aren't obscured, and the well-made grits make the dish stick to your ribs. Most accounts of the origin of the rise of shrimp and grits as a southern restaurant staple point to Craig Claiborne's piece in the New York Times *about enjoying the dish at Crook's Corner, Bill Neal's restaurant in Chapel Hill, North Carolina. Both of these southerners have influenced countless cooks throughout the United States, so it's no wonder that shrimp and grits has proliferated. This shrimp and grits recipe is an attempt to return the dish to its roots.*

FOR THE GRITS

2 cups whole milk

2 cups water

6 tablespoons unsalted butter

1 teaspoon kosher salt

1 teaspoon freshly ground black pepper

1 cup stone-ground grits

½ cup grated sharp cheddar cheese

FOR THE GRAVY

12 tablespoons unsalted butter

½ pound smoked hog jowls, julienned

¾ cup all-purpose flour

2 cups thinly sliced yellow onions

1 tablespoon Creole seasoning (page 26)

4 cups chicken broth

1 teaspoon thyme

½ teaspoon kosher salt

1 tablespoon parsley

½ cup chopped green onions

FOR THE SHRIMP

2 pounds large shrimp (21/25), peeled

1 tablespoon kosher salt

2 tablespoons unsalted butter

1 pound andouille sausage, cut in half and sliced

4 tablespoons chopped green onions

To make the grits, combine the milk, water, butter, salt, and pepper in a heavy-bottomed saucepan and bring to a boil. Reduce the heat to a simmer and stir in the grits. Stir continuously with a wire whisk to keep the grits from clumping. Once all of the grits are blended, continue to stir for 2–3 minutes. Reduce the heat and cook for 15–20 minutes, stirring periodically with a wooden spoon. Remove from the heat and stir in the cheese.

To make the gravy, melt the butter in a cast-iron skillet over medium-high heat and add the hog jowls to render the fat. Remove the rendered hog jowls with a slotted spoon and reserve. Add the flour to the butter and stir constantly until it turns a hazelnut brown color. Be careful—this mixture can burn if you stop stirring, and if splashed onto your skin, it will cause a serious burn. Add the yellow onions and continue stirring. Again, be careful—onions have lots of water in them, and adding them to a hot pan creates steam, which can burn your hand. When the onions look brown and wilted, add the reserved hog jowls and Creole seasoning; cook for 5 minutes or so, stirring regularly to distribute the seasoning. Add the chicken broth, thyme, and salt; bring to a simmer and cook for 10 minutes, or until thickened. Taste to see if the flour flavor has dissipated; if not, simmer 5 minutes longer. Remove from the heat and stir in the parsley and green onions.

To make the shrimp, season them with the salt. Heat the butter in a heavy-bottomed Dutch oven or cast-iron skillet. Add the sausage and sauté until lightly browned and rendered. Add the shrimp and sauté until hot throughout. Add the gravy, toss to coat, and heat throughout.

Divide the grits between 4 bowls and top with the shrimp mixture. Garnish with the green onions.

Acknowledgments

This book would not have been possible without the dedication of my lovely wife, Morgan—"You make me real; strong as I feel, you make me reel." Several folks read a rough draft of the manuscript and pointed me in the right direction: David Bailey, Sheri Castle, Nancie McDermott, John Shelton Reed, Maureen Downey, and Felicia McMillan. Lee Healy, how do I get through a day without you setting me straight? Elaine Maisner, thanks for giving me a chance. Paula Wald, thank you for crossing the "t"s and dotting the "i"s. I read a few books to help with the historical angle: *Hard Times and a Nickel a Bucket* (2004) by John R. Maiolo; *Texas Shrimpers* (1983) by Robert Lee Maril; and *Shrimp Cookery* (1952) by Helen Worth. My mom and dad, Collette Boudreaux and William Pierce, taught me to love making a roux and AC/DC, both of which are instrumental to cooking. Too many wonderful chefs to name here have generously guided me along the path I've been traveling the last twenty years, but you'll find some hints in the recipe headnotes. Esma Richoux Trosclair, I channel you— the food and the attitude. Not least, Andrew and Sydney inspire me each day to be a better teacher and a more loving dad.

Index

Appetizers. *See* Small plates

Bacon-Wrapped Shrimp Brochettes with Rhubarbecue Sauce, 16
Brandied Shrimp Bisque, 58
Buttered Brown Rice with Shrimp, Duck Cracklings, and Roasted Mushrooms, 88

Cajun Shrimp Boil, 102
Calabash Cajun Carbonara, 76
Classic Fried Shrimp Po'boys, 64
Coconut Fried Shrimp with Mango-Teriyaki Sauce, 34
Creamed Rice with Spicy Sausage and Shrimp, 86
Cream of Fennel Soup with Shrimp, 50

Esma's Shrimp Stew, 94

Fire-Roasted Shrimp Tacos, 66

Garlicky Shrimp with Angel Hair Pasta, 74
Grilled Shrimp Caesar Salad, 40
Grilled Steaks with Shrimp Butter, 104
Gulf Shrimp Rolls, 68

Jambalaya, 82

Lemony Shrimp Risotto, 90

Main dishes, 99
Buttered Brown Rice with Shrimp, Duck Cracklings, and Roasted Mushrooms, 88
Cajun Shrimp Boil, 102
Calabash Cajun Carbonara, 76
Classic Fried Shrimp Po'boys, 64
Creamed Rice with Spicy Sausage and Shrimp, 86
Fire-Roasted Shrimp Tacos, 66
Garlicky Shrimp with Angel Hair Pasta, 74
Grilled Steaks with Shrimp Butter, 104
Gulf Shrimp Rolls, 68
Jambalaya, 82
Lemony Shrimp Risotto, 90
Shrimp and Grits, 109
Shrimp and Okra, 92
Shrimp and Spinach Enchiladas, 100
Shrimp Burgers with Boiler Room Tartar Sauce, Tomatoes, and Arugula, 70
Shrimp Country Captain, 84
Shrimp Étouffée, 96
Shrimp Linguine, 78
Shrimp-Stuffed Pork Chops, 106
Mirliton and Shrimp Soup, 52

New Orleans–Style Barbecue Shrimp in South Carolina, 36

Popcorn Shrimp Rémoulade Salad, 42
Prized Pickled Shrimp, 33

Roasted Shrimp Salad, 45
Rosemary Shrimp and White
    Bean Soup, 56

Salads, 39
    Grilled Shrimp Caesar Salad,
        40
    Popcorn Shrimp Rémoulade
        Salad, 42
    Roasted Shrimp Salad, 45
    Shrimp and Peach Salad, 44
Salt-and-Pepper Shrimp, 18
Saucy Cocktail with Shrimp, 26
Seafood Gumbo, 48
Shrimp: frozen, 9; how to freeze,
    12; pairing with beverages,
    12–14; peeling and devein-
    ing, 9; quality identifiers,
    11–12; sizes of, 10–11; wild-
    caught vs. farm-raised, 7–9
Shrimp and Grits, 109
Shrimp and Leek Quiche, 20
Shrimp and Okra, 92
Shrimp and Peach Salad, 44
Shrimp and Spinach Enchiladas,
    100
Shrimp Aspic, 30
Shrimp Burgers with Boiler
    Room Tartar Sauce,
    Tomatoes, and Arugula, 70
Shrimp Ceviche, 28
Shrimp Country Captain, 84
Shrimp Étouffée, 96
Shrimp Linguine, 78
Shrimp Omelet, 32
Shrimp-Stuffed Pork Chops, 106
Shrimp with Cocktail Sauce, 24
Small plates, 15
    Bacon-Wrapped Shrimp
        Brochettes with
        Rhubarbecue Sauce, 16
    Bertie County Company
        Shrimp and Crackers, 22
    Coconut Fried Shrimp with
        Mango-Teriyaki Sauce, 34
    New Orleans–Style Barbecue
        Shrimp in South Carolina,
        36
    Prized Pickled Shrimp, 33
    Salt-and-Pepper Shrimp, 18
    Saucy Cocktail with Shrimp,
        26
    Shrimp and Leek Quiche, 20
    Shrimp Aspic, 30
    Shrimp Ceviche, 28
    Shrimp Omelet, 32
    Shrimp with Cocktail Sauce, 24
Soups and Stews, 47
    Brandied Shrimp Bisque, 58
    Cream of Fennel Soup with
        Shrimp, 50
    Esma's Shrimp Stew, 94
    Mirliton and Shrimp Soup, 52
    Rosemary Shrimp and White
        Bean Soup, 56
    Seafood Gumbo, 48
    Southwestern Shrimp Stew,
        108
    Sweet Potato Soup with Ginger
        Shrimp, 60
    Tom Yum Goong, a Thai
        Shrimp Soup, 54
Southwestern Shrimp Stew, 108
Sweet Potato Soup with Ginger
    Shrimp, 60

Tom Yum Goong, a Thai Shrimp
    Soup, 54

Printed in the USA
CPSIA information can be obtained
at www.ICGtesting.com
CBHW081635180224
4434CB00013B/422